The Maestro
MONOLOGUE

discover your genius
defeat your intruder
design your destiny

The Mind Adventure Inc.

The Mind Adventure Inc. – robwhite180@gmail.com

ISBN: 978-0-578-87570-5 (print)
ISBN: 978-0-578-87571-2 (ebook)

Ordering Information:
Special discounts are available on quantity purchases by corporations, associations, and others. For details, contact us at robwhitemedia.com or at robwhite180@gmail.com.

The Maestro
MONOLOGUE

discover your genius
defeat your intruder
design your destiny

ROB WHITE

For all of you who seek
a greater understanding
of the extraordinary resources
that come with being a human being.

Contents

Part Three:
High Spirits as
You Are Revealed

Part Four:
Thy Kingdom Come

Beware the *Intruder*

IT'S TRICKY

Grab hold, you are about to awaken to what you "already know" about yourself, but aren't yet aware that you know. This awakening opens you to deeper dimensions of your remarkably resourceful nature, which empowers you to be "the source" of how your life unfolds.

When it comes to orchestrating your life—you are the Maestro! You are a unique one-of-a-kind individual, born to think for yourself and born to live for yourself. If you're to experience that, you must be *true* to yourself.

However, it's not that simple.

In fact, it's tricky, and that's because there's an *intruder* vying for first-place position in your consciousness.

Yes, the Maestro has competition.

This *intruder* is an unwanted mental houseguest that stops you from conducting your daily affairs fruitfully, so your life can unfold like the beautiful symphony it's meant to be.

Warning: this book is hazardous to the *intruder's* health.

Your opportunity has come to take up your rightful position as the Maestro. When you do that you create an incredible relationship with the most important person in your life: your authentic self.

Are you ready to achieve supreme insights into the true nature of your being, so you may think for yourself and experience the life you dream of living?

Are you feeling *stuck* in any area of your life right now? The exercises in this book are designed to help you overcome the emotional barriers that muddle your mind and stifle your enthusiasm. Those barriers are the doings of the *intruder*. Feel free to modify the exercises so they speak directly to you. Those you modify will prove to be the most illuminating.

The reading pace is comfortable, all information is offered in bite-sized pieces and is easily digestible. There are no complex concepts to grasp, no intellectual hoops to jump through. You'll experience a sensitivity of flow from chapter to chapter, which makes it easy to cruise through the book.

Along with parables, metaphors, and stories, there are also many inspiring quotes from sages of the past that will help you discover and recover your many remarkable resources in restorative ways. These active thinkers, scholars, and philosophers are my "coauthors." On occasion, I interpret their teachings and reflections in my own fashion. Their insights and my interpretations will help stir the oracle within you, and that's when, like sudden flashes of lightning, your own insights will mysteriously appear. These experiences will come in proportion to your readiness to receive them.

There is rhythm and measured repetition that enables the information to sink deeper into your consciousness, and replace wrong thinking with right perception.

And one more thing: if you are to experience the kind of world in which you'd love to reside, you need one person on your side—YOU!

> Trust the truth.
> Relax.
> Take time to reflect.
> Have fun.
> Pack lightly.
> Remain curious.
> Be ready for surprises.

Walt Whitman spoke a profound truism when he aptly chose the words: "I am not contain'd between my hat and boots."[1]

> Put on your boots.
> Hold on to your hat.
> Cinch your seatbelt.
> You have been forewarned.
> This book will have an impact…

The Setup

BE PREPARED

Right now, you are standing center stage in the theater of your life. The timing is perfect. You wouldn't be reading this book if it wasn't. No one can walk your path on your behalf. Be prepared to shatter all the myths, superstitions, misconceptions, and negative opinions that have hampered you from experiencing your unique, one-of-a-kind authenticity. It's in this alert state that you are able to banish what inhibits you from realizing your unrealized potential.

> You were *not* born too early.
> You were *not* born too late.
> You were *not* born into the wrong family.
> You were *not* born into the wrong community.

It matters not your age, IQ, education, religious affiliation, or political persuasion—you are consummate possibility. This is *your* time to realize who you always have been—the Maestro—ever ready to fashion your life into a beautiful symphony.

> You *were* born to be healthy.
> You *were* born to be happy.
> You *were* born to be successful.
> You *were* born to love and to be loved.
> You *were* born to be in service in outstanding ways.

It was errors in self-judgment, made in childhood moments of failure and fear, that gave the *intruder* a life in your life. This trespasser carries with him many kegs of psychological dynamite that repeatedly blow your dreams to smithereens—those dreams of winning in life, in relationships, in business, with experiences of gratitude, love and joy.

As we journey together through these pages, you will learn, one way after another, how to dismantle those kegs of dynamite, and rid yourself of this imposter, pretending to be you.

Your greatest gains occur as you come to realize that you already know all you need to know to free yourself from the *intruder's* psychological blows. What if you were to live into the full possibility for what life could be for you, and took complete responsibility for that? When you do that, there's nothing that can stop you from becoming your personal best.

THE MAP

Imagine, if you will, a stranger approaches you with a treasure map and tells you, "The map I'm holding will show you the way to the kingdom in which your heart yearns to dwell, a place where you're free to reveal yourself as infinite possibility, like you felt as a child, once again."

All children intuitively know they are overflowing with talent and oozing with potential, and they fully intended to express it. However, things happened, and they forget all about it.

This stranger is offering you the opportunity to remember what you forgot, but then he tears the map into four pieces and tosses them into the wind!

Would you collect the four pieces?

Great!

Be glad.

I have gathered the pieces and put them together for you. This book is your treasure map. It holds exactly what you need to see yourself as a source of unlimited resources so you can create the life you dream of living. What you find will be both spell-breaking and spellbinding.

Part One is the heartthrob.

In this part of the journey, you travel to the land of the *Ultimate Understanding*. This understanding brings remarkable new ways of seeing yourself into perspective.

New ways of seeing yourself offer you new ways of being yourself, and new ways of being yourself open you to a future with untold new possibilities. That's when you begin noticing new opportunities to orchestrate your life as you want it to be.

Part Two explains why the heart stops throbbing.

Here we trek into the world where the *intruder* dwells—the imposter that has played 10,000 underhanded tricks on you. This part of the journey teaches you how to deal with this uninvited guest and *its* anxious, reactive behavior. That's when you begin to take charge and scare *its* scares away.

Part Three introduces you to the *Maestro Monologue.*

With the Maestro Monologue, your heart starts throbbing with eager anticipation. This narrative reacquaints you with three remarkably resourceful states of being that await your attention. These states give you access to greater dimensions of successful living than you've ever envisioned.

After completing Part Three, never again will you forget what is ultimately true about you, which goes far beyond what your usual reasoning mind can offer you.

Part Four takes you to the magic kingdom.

You have arrived home at last! This is the paradise you've always been seeking—and it's right in your own backyard. There are two exceptional advantages you'll find here, which validate all the good and beautiful things you'll have discovered about yourself.

CHIP, CHIP, CHIP

This journey is *not* about *adding* anything new to who you already are. That's because there's nothing missing. It's about *subtracting* what you are *not*. For it's with subtraction that you uncover what's hidden.

Venus de Milo would have forever remained a secret if Alexandros of Antioch did not chip, chip, chip away at that chunk of marble. Get ready

[handwritten margin note: In Christ we already have all things]

to start chipping away at your layers of faulty self-opinions, so your own unique Venus de Milo no longer remains a secret to you.

As you begin chipping away at what's causing you so much confusion, your memory is jogged and you nudge yourself awake to remarkable truths that you'd forgotten about yourself long ago.

Whoosh! It's like stepping out of a dark cave into bright light. Sweet release! You are in for an extraordinary experience.

You are going to fall in love with yourself, once again, like you felt when you were just learning to walk and talk, intuitively knowing that you were overflowing with talent and oozing with potential.

This journey is an adventure of inner rebellion during which you extract raw truths about yourself in ways that feel like déjà vu—yet they'll feel exciting and new. It's not far into the book before you begin experiencing subtle shifts in consciousness, and all manner of wisdom and passion will begin rushing to you.

> Prepare yourself.
> Life is benevolent.
> Life never blinks.
> Life is always responding to what you think.

By the time you've turned the final page of this book you will have created a thousand opportunities for new possibilities in your life. Never again will you be ignorant of your astounding capacities, and never again will you lower your sights on what you expect from yourself.

You are now launching yourself on a journey that begins your self-rescue, which will lead to a freedom of expression experienced by few...

"Sweet Release" that was going to be the name of my first book, years (it years ago!

PART ONE

understanding what's
ultimately true about you

chapter 1

Awareness Training

YOUR UNDERSTANDINGS

Your life is the way it is because you are the way you are. And you are the way you are because of how you understand yourself to be. There is no better way to mark an end to an era and initiate a new beginning than by studying how you understand yourself to be.

You are a remarkable subject deserving of such study. Furthermore, who is better qualified to study *you* than you? When you consciously study yourself with ruthless honesty, you create openings to understand yourself very differently. And when you change what it means to be you, your entire life changes.

You always think as you think and act as you act because of what you always understand to be true about you. I am referring to those points of view that you hold tightly to. Those are the understandings that literally *call you to be*. They give you your "presence" in the world.

Your usual understandings give you that feeling of familiarity that you're comfortable with, when out there in the world with others and when you're alone with yourself. Those are your typical moods, recurring attitudes, and everyday expressions.

How you understand yourself to be gives you your concerns in the world. And so it goes, if you understood yourself differently, your concerns would be different, and your responses to the circumstances in your life would be different.

If you have any notion that there are powers outside of you that give you the kind of world you experience, let that notion be shaken thoroughly. You've put your world together from how you've put yourself together. And you've put yourself together from what you've come to understand to be true about yourself.

If we take this a step further, it becomes apparent that you don't live "in the world," but rather you've created a world that lives in you, and what you understand about your world is always congruent with what you understand about yourself.

It can be no other way—your world is a mirror! It continually validates your opinions about yourself by reflecting back to you what you are projecting outwardly. There's no avoiding it—you act the way you act in the world because of how you understand yourself to be, hence you reap from your world what your understandings sow.

THE WORLD FREELY OFFERS ITSELF

The world is life-friendly, it *freely* offers itself to you, it has no strings attached. However, because you don't respond directly to what's happening in the world, but rather, you respond from your understandings—the world can only serve you as you direct it to. It's your world!

No matter how scientific or diligent you may be when collecting, analyzing, and organizing data about your world, your self-understandings can have an impact on your interpretations and explanations of the world that are very different from the facts.

The dust is beginning to settle.

Your self-understandings are incredibly powerful. They give you what you *stand for*. And what you *stand for*, you *stand up for* with your attitudes and moods. And what you *stand up for*, you *stand under* and support with your everyday expressions.

Your many dispositions are revealings and validations of your many understandings. When you look deeply into those understandings that influence you most, you've touched upon the wellspring of beliefs that make you *you*! Your undying loyalty to those beliefs give you your experiences of yourself in the world.

We assume that our understandings of ourselves come from valid observations of ourselves in the world. However, what we fail to realize is that we make ourselves into our understandings first, and then we go out into the world and justify those understanding by acting in ways that validate them. Then we say, "This is just the way I am."

We've gone deep in a short period of time.

As it becomes more and more apparent to you that your action in the world is a direct correlate to how the world occurs to you, and it occurs to you according to how you occur to yourself in the world—your world starts to make sense.

Pretty powerful stuff, eh?

YOUR PERSONALITY

Your personality is an important piece to all of this. Your personality is your personal harp, from which you play your tunes. Your tunes contain your moods, your emotions, your feelings, and all those charming little quirks that make you *you*.

If you take the time to study your personality, you will find all your understandings about yourself and those mutually related cravings, fears, and ambitions all right there, ready to be expressed at the drop of a hat.

When your expressions are satisfying, your responses in the world are gratifying. That's because you're communicating from an understanding of yourself that is pleasing.

However, when your expression is upsetting, that's because your understanding of yourself is upsetting you, hence, you *are an upset waiting to happen*. And when you communicate from that point of view, you set yourself up to be upset. Hence, it shows up in your action, and your world inevitably proves to be upsetting to you.

Your personality—your personal harp and your tunes—are uniquely yours, like your fingerprints. They determine the kind of work you do, the kinds of friends you make, the kinds of hobbies you have, and the kinds of vacations you take.

Your task, on this adventure, is to distinguish between the two personalities available to you and the understandings that support each of them, and then deal with them effectively.

It's a giant step to accept that it's *not* the circumstances in your world, but rather your understandings about yourself that determine your life experiences. It's an even bigger step to be willing to admit that perhaps many of your understanding about yourself have missed the mark.

MISS-UNDERSTANDING

If you're to be a source of ongoing joy and satisfaction for yourself, it's vital that you appreciate the power that your understandings wield. And more crucial than that is to distinguish between those understandings that *are* valid and those that are *not*.

Oftentimes, in order to grow, it's necessary to study what shocks you. In this case, it's important to look at your understandings that are *not true*, those understandings about yourself that miss the mark. I call those understandings your *miss-understandings*.

It's important to get that your *miss-understandings* shape and form your personality just as much as those understandings that are true.

Do you suspect that you may be accomplishing but a fraction of what's possible for you? Let this moment be a launching point to begin proving your suspicion correct. Remain suspicious. Your wariness will help you discover those *miss-understandings* that have harmed you.

Coming to understand how you've come to understand yourself as you do will take you on a wet and wild adventure. Did you bring your inflatable life vest? We will address this matter in many ways as we journey through this book together.

The first question we inevitably ask ourselves when anything new happens in our world, is this: "What does this have to do with me?" We either ask it consciously or unconsciously.

Unfortunately, there are two awfully popular follow-up questions we learn to ask ourselves when things aren't going as we want them to. These questions are found in all cultures, and they set the whole human family spinning in the direction of *an upset waiting to happen*. The questions are these: "What's *wrong* here?" And what often follows that is, "What's *wrong* with me?" The second question is a trap! We think it's a valid question, but it's not.

If you find yourself asking the second question for any reason—know there is most definitely something *wrong*! However, it's *not* something wrong with *you*; it's something very wrong with the *question*! It sets you up for many *miss-understandings*. Oh, what a mistake you make when you take

What's wrong with me?!
TOXIC
thought

that question personally! That one question feeds into psychological fears that make you underappreciate ourselves immensely.

All of humanity's *miss-understandings* are derivatives of the toxic question, *"What's wrong with me?"* Consequently, the answers we come to put extreme limits on what we do, which limits us from realizing our incredible potential.

Are you prepared to plunge deeply into the self-understandings you live with, so you can understand what drives your every concern and action? By looking directly at how you've put yourself together, you open up space for impressive breakthroughs that offer remarkable opportunities to eliminate a thousand *miss-understandings* and emotional judgments you're holding about yourself; judgments that do damage to your health and happiness.

premise of book

READY YOURSELF

You've stepped onto the playing field and are now standing dead square in the conversation of this book.

You are now in awareness training. If you remain curious on this quest for truth, you are going to find yourself continually awakening, not once but twice:

- First, you'll awaken to strong, but *wrong* understandings that you've arrived at about yourself.
- Second, you'll awaken with energy-releasing enthusiasm to the truth of your limitless nature.

 # 1 Over your life, you've catalogued thousands of understandings about yourself. Those that are accurate point to the remarkable wealth of resources that comes with *being* a human being *Child of God*. Those that miss the mark blind you from seeing the truth about your immeasurable potential.

Unfortunately, understandings, be they accurate or inaccurate, are powerful forces of energy that work diligently to perpetuate themselves.

You'll be wearing X-ray glasses throughout this expedition—glasses that help you see straight through those *miss-understandings* that blind you to the truth. When you develop a fascination with distinguishing your accurate understandings from your *miss-understandings*, the more clearly you're able to see how you've (unwittingly) created yourself to be. And the more accepting you become to the truth about yourself, the less accepting you are to *miss-understandings* that lead you astray.

Hear ye the good news!

One of the great perks that comes with being a human being is that you have the capacity to make corrections to rid yourself of toxic understandings that poison your personality. And the best way to make corrections is by asking healthy questions.

HEALTHY QUESTIONS

Productive results come from healthy questions because healthy questions are the foundation for new understandings that set you up for new possibilities. Furthermore, when you make a habit of asking in that manner, you develop your muscle for asking even better questions, which give you access to even better answers—answers offering you greater depths of joy and vitality.

A vital piece of this journey is to learn to ask healthy questions. A healthy question is radically different than the unhealthy question like, *"What's wrong with me?"* A healthy question creates a clearings for a healthy attitude. This sets you up for new points of view, which can prove to be the most powerful antidote to what emotionally ails you.

Here's an example of a healthy question to substitute for *"What's wrong with me?"* Simply ask yourself, *"How might I see myself differently so I might learn something that empowers me?"* Ask that question meaningfully, and it immediately expands your view to include possibilities that you couldn't see with the prior question.

You'll be amazed at the problems you can solve when you counsel yourself wisely by having a healthy question or two handy. Have your pen and paper ready; there are tons of healthy questions coming your way on this journey.

If you're to loosen the grip your *miss-understandings* have on you, it's important you stop insisting that you "already understand all there is to understand about yourself." Can you see the problem that arises when that's what you insist? Are you willing to let go of such arrogance? Every tip in this book can be personally tested and proven true by you.

ZERO LIMITS

The only way to give your limitless potential the respect it deserves is to explore more and more of the infinite unknown about you. There are zero limits to how far you can go!

If you were to aspire a little higher right now, with no *miss-understandings* to handicap you, what would be your desire?

Financial prosperity?
More love in your life?
More satisfaction at work?
More fulfilling relationships?

It's your turn: _*financial resources/more love,*_

(Did you jot down your desire? You've got to engage if these exercises are to help you explore more.)

When *miss-understandings* are dealt with properly, they lead to higher realms of accurate understandings that always strengthen you. Imagine fearlessly committing to diving deeper into the truth about yourself, unencumbered by any *miss-understanding* that try to stop you.

Here's a taste of what's coming: as you dive deeper into your *miss-understandings*, you will encounter that unwanted mental guest—the *intruder*—that has moved in and taken over. When the *intruder* is in charge, you can be sure your emotions will push you right off the edge of a cliff every time.

As you become fully acquainted with the *intruder* and its many kegs of dynamite that blow your dreams to smithereens, you'll find yourself shifting your whole world on its axis. That's when you begin identifying and correcting those *miss-understandings* that fuel this imposter pretending to be you. We will cover this pernicious peculiarity in detail in part two of this book.

By the end of this exploration, you'll have served an eviction notice to that unwanted mental border, and immediately you gain access to many remarkable powers you've always possessed but forgot all about.

Let me introduce you to two powers that you'll be calling upon immediately.

IMMOBILIZING AND MONOPOLIZING

Your ability to *immobilize your focus* is a power of great value. With one healthy question you can confine your mind to a single intention. And with your focus immobilized, you awaken another valuable power—your ability to *monopolize your attention.* When your attention is consumed, you are no longer led astray by distractions, and that's when the fog lifts!

Without the polestars of *immobilized focus* and *monopolized attention*, your mind spirals randomly, causing flustering emotions that make it impossible to make necessary corrections. This expedition is designed to immobilize your focus and monopolize your attention, with the intention of replacing self-deception with empowering self-perception.

Your capacity to turn your life in the direction that you want it to go is incalculable. Imagine waking up every morning with an inviting smile on your face, eager to jump into your day. Let's make that real for you. If you stay with me all the way through, and engage in the questions and exercises offered, and if you don't give up even when it's frustrating—this will open you to levels of thinking where you will no longer feel bound up by invalid, albeit familiar, points of view that have been stifling you. That's when you'll feel fully alive, knowing life is a privilege!

There's your power!

If you're to truly take advantage of what we're up to together, it's important that you continually test this stuff out for yourself. The litmus tests will prove positive as you learn more and more ways to *immobilize* and *monopolize* in order to stabilize your visions of victory and take command of your destiny.

Brace yourself. With what you've read so far, you are already creating openings to participate in life in ways that give presence to your magnificence. It won't be long before you make an astonishing distinction: "My gosh, it is true! *I am the Maestro* when it comes to orchestrating my life!"

It's time to introduce you to another awesome power that is always available to you. A power that enables you to abruptly interrupt any *miss-understanding* that has you careening down a negative stream…

chapter 2

An Astonishing Power

THE POWER OF INTERVENTION

You are endowed with an awesome power—the Power of Intervention. This power creates a clearing for self-renewal. It enables you to turn your thoughts in the right direction when your self-talk is fraught with faulty ruminations. When you use this power productively you begin noticing the many opinions you hold of yourself that just ain't so, and realize it's time to let them go.

Your outer world is an event that is always luring you to engage, but it's the state of your inner world that determines the course of action you take. It's the reckless chattering of erroneous assumptions that prevents you from engaging in a constructive fashion. The Power of Intervention puts you in an authoritative position, so you can put an end to that chatter.

Your actions are *not* responses to what's happening in the outer world, they are responses to what's happening in your inner world. Your inner world requires continual monitoring because that's where your understandings and *miss-understandings* are found, which are the real source of your actions.

When you use your Power of Intervention to effectively free yourself of your *miss-understandings*, you see yourself as a valuable and contributing force in life, and your actions reflect that. When you see yourself as anything less than that, your responses are feeble. That's a call to action—it's time to intervene in your inner world by interrupting your inner dialogue.

Nervously reacting is a consequence of an inner narrative that is self-demeaning. Such a narrative gives you a very narrow range of choices when it comes to participating in life. In such moments it's always appropriate to interrupt.

The moment you release your Power of Intervention onto any self-degrading inner discourse, you immediately alter the way you occur to yourself, which immediately alters the way the world occurs to you. Inevitably, that alters your action in the world.

When your world occurs as threatening, it's because you occur to yourself as inadequate, which is a consequence of a degrading inner dialogue. You never, never, never need to bear the brunt of belittling opinions that have been programmed into your nervous system. The only way to deal with this is to tackle it head on by intervening.

Your feelings of inadequacy began when you began listening to your *miss-understandings*. There's not one opinion that corrupts your mood or sours your attitude that need be a permanent fixture in your belief system! All such points of view are correctable.

Your Power of Intervention is key to your success in life. Learning how to harness this power for your own good can be transformational. You are on your way to learning how to use this power with all matters big and small.

UNLIMITED POSSIBILITIES

Being human comes with unlimited possibility, however, our reasons for failing at our aspirations blind us to that fact. Most of our reasons come from our *miss-understandings*. When we use our Power of Intervention productively, we cast aside those *miss-understandings* and get to the bottom of things. That's when we see possibilities, beyond what our reasons offer.

Ergo, you must think for yourself if you are to experience yourself as unlimited possibility. When you set yourself on that track you'll find yourself advancing a lot farther a lot faster, and you'll see no reason whatsoever to go back.

Do you know the one thing that can prevent you from setting yourself straight when your inner narrative is giving you a nervous ache? It's *your own resistance* to your incredible potential. When you release your Power of Intervention onto correcting your resistance, there is no stopping you.

18

Your life becomes a remarkable adventure when you use your Power of Intervention to discriminate between *miss-understandings* that need eliminating and understandings that nourish you so you can be sharp, strong, and swift of mind.

Imagine challenging all those reasons you rely upon to justify your *supposed shortcomings*. It's time to be rigorously honest with yourself. It's time to begin noticing the many veils of *miss-understandings* you've layered over the incredible truth about yourself.

O&O

We human beings are unpredictable critters for sure. We are Herculean when we use our creative energy befittingly, and yet how quickly we turn that energy upside down and let it bounce us around.

We love reflecting on ourselves, however when we turn those reflections into ruminations of ruin, we do ourselves great harm.

One grave error we make when we ruminate over a mistake, is to *Overemphasize* our assumptions of being deficient. If only it stopped there. The next thing we do is *Overapply* our nervous reactions, which reinforces our faulty assumptions.

The two negative tendencies of *Overemphasizing* and *Overapplying*—O&O—are powerful fortifiers of *miss-understandings*, which cause more problems. Can you remember a time when you overemphasized your opinion of being deficient? Can you remember overapplying your feeling of anxiety when you reacted? What did you expect to achieve, and what benefit did you expect to receive when you did that?

A perfect first step to resolving this problem is understanding how this process works.

JOHN

"I know I'm way too heavy," John sobs. "But screw it; there's *nothing* I can do about it. I'm big-boned, and I have a slow metabolism."

John then polishes off a half gallon of rocky road ice cream, out of misaligned frustration and resignation.

John's feelings, thoughts, and actions all match up perfectly with how he occurs to himself—hopeless and helpless. Can you see any *exaggeration* in John's situation?

What if John were to release his Power of Intervention onto his self-talk by asking this healthy question: "Is it possible I'm *overemphasizing my inability to lose weight?*" Productive change begins when John begins speaking to himself in a productive manner. With that one question, John has the opportunity to take command of his inner world and alter how he occurs to himself. That's the Power of Intervention in action!

The Power of Intervention combined with a healthy question brings light to any dark situation.

What if John intervened further by agreeing that he'd *overapplied* his frustrated reaction by eating a half gallon of ice cream? Right there, John has opened his mind a crack to learn something new about his overweight condition. A shift in attitude like this—from helpless to hopeful—can shift the whole realm of possibilities in which John exists! Remarkable recoveries come in moments like this.

If you're to learn what's right and true about you, it's important that you learn what *ain't* right and *ain't* true, so you can intervene when you're *overemphasizing* those *miss-understandings* that lead you to *overapplying* your nervous reaction.

> "Come to the edge," he said.
> "We can't, we're afraid!" they responded.
> "Come to the edge," he said.
> "We can't, we will fall!" they responded.
> "Come to the edge," he said.
>   And so they came.
>   And he pushed them.
>   And they flew.
>
> —Christopher Logue[2]

The strong wings of a fledgling are useless if the fledgling *overemphasizes* her inability to use them. With the opinion, "I can't, I will fall!" the fledgling *overreacts* by gripping tightly to the branch of the tree upon which she is perched. That branch is your "comfort zone," which offers you no growth, if you look closely.

When it's time to take flight, never allow negative rhetoric to dominate your inner narrative, forcing you to cling to a low branch on the tree of life.

REMARKABLE ELIXIRS

There's no better way to intervene, when stuck in a mood of resignation, than to ask a healthy question that offers you the opportunity to deal with the limiting decisions you've come to about yourself.

Healthy questions are helpful questions that offer elixirs. With those kinds of questions you're fly-fishing for new possibilities, and you never know what empowering insight may grab the bait!

> Okay, let's do an exercise together.
> Take a moment to fetch your pen.
> I'll wait.
> Wow, that was quick.
> Are you ready?

In what area of your life do you fear to launch into flight? *Sales of any kind... my services, my knowledge, my products (think outside sales) etc.*

What's the reason you're stuck, as you see it? *that I can't follow through, or it'll be too sales-y, people will think I'm just trying to make a dollar.*

Is it possible the reason is a product of a *miss-understanding* you're holding onto? A *miss-understanding* that makes you feel incapable in the face of this condition? Is it possible you're *overemphasizing* that *miss-understanding*? *that I'm desperate*

What is your usual reaction when you are feeling stuck with this condition? *that I just take my "backseat" way out + let excuses rule!*

Is it possible you are *overapplying* that reaction?

If you're alive, you're qualified to live a fabulous life! Hence, you are qualified! You are now pinpointing those *miss-understandings* and subsequent reactions that stop you from living a fabulous life.

(You did engage in the exercise by answering the questions, didn't you?)

Your mental chatter always matters! When you berate yourself, you dam up your natural outpouring of enthusiasm and curiosity. Dare to intervene when you catch yourself in that scene. And what better way to intervene than to step beyond the mechanics of your reactive mind by asking yourself a question that challenges the ordinary? *why do I think I shouldn't sell a product + make money off of it?*

Your Power of Intervention is an incredible asset. Who knows what might happen if you exercise this power daily? Perhaps those lofty goals you forgot about yesterday are awaiting your approval today?

Before we go any further, it's important to point out that aspiring to fly higher, and then intervening when your self-talk is demeaning does not guarantee success.

INTERVENING WITH NEW MEANING

Your flight through life will most assuredly include experiences of losing. Being human is about winning some and losing some and learning from our losses. Losing doesn't make you a loser. If you think you're a loser, you can't learn from your losses. The only way to ultimately win is to lose and learn, and progress once again. Evolution requires that of you.

A life of growth is, by nature, a life of mistakes. The mistakes are fundamental to your involvement in your *evolvement*. Hence, your every mistake offers possibility! The perfect way to handle feeling deficient after making a mistake, is to intervene with a new meaning for the word.

Call it a "*miss-take.*"

When you call your errors "*miss-takes,*" you are agreeing that you *missed the mark*, and at the same time you are highlighting the importance of learning something so you can refine what you did. However, when you see your mistakes as complaints, now you've created a problem. You feel defeated.

Two invitations come with mistakes: (1) *miss-takes* as opportunities to learn something and (2) mistakes as problems to complain about. Seeing your *miss-takes* as opportunities requires self-responsibility, so necessary corrections become a probability rather than a rarity.

There's no better way to develop an exciting relationship with your losses than to make a habit of extracting lessons from those *miss-takes*. *Miss-takes* are remarkably useful when you stop considering them "evidence" of your supposed inadequacies. More action, more mistakes, more life lessons learned.

Growing and glowing are a consequence of knowing that mistakes are *miss-takes* requiring refinement. Refine your action and enjoy a successful *re-take*. Then acknowledge your victory: "Hooray! *That's a take!*" Speak it like a movie director does, after successfully refining a scene.

Sailing a boat into the wind is a perfect example of *miss-take, re-take, miss-take, re-take...* "*That's a take!*" Zig-zagging off-course, on-course, off-course, on-course—until you arrive at your destination. In the sailing world it's called tacking; in human development you could call it "failing forward".

What sweet fantasy might you take seriously if you didn't make a federal case of your mistakes? When you tune into the mindset of *miss-takes,* your failures become stepping-stones, rather than stumbling blocks to mumble and grumble about.

Imagine making a habit of seeing your *miss-takes* as opportunities to refine your thinking. Suddenly, those put-down messages become blurred ink as you claim sovereignty over faulty conversations that stifle your creative expression.

Calling a mistake a "*miss-take*" is an ideal way to intervene when you catch yourself *overemphasizing* and *overapplying* your feeling of disappointment and thoughts of ineptness after making an error. The knowledge you gain from refining your thought-theme offers you great leverage over any bad attitude that may show up. That one move helps you to cut straight through the jungle of *miss-understandings* that cause you so many problems.

Your willingness to intervene on negative thought-themes is the beginning of serial breakthroughs to the truth of your unstoppable nature. The path to personal growth requires we stop insisting that we already understand all there is to understand about ourselves. Your reasoning mind, with its intelligent theories and thousands of excuses, will never understand the truth of your *limitless* potential if you maintain that attitude.

> When you make a *miss-take* and put yourself down,
> You feel like a fragile leaf,
> Clinging to a limb on a tree
> As the winds of self-doubt shake you about.

You are the ruler of your mental kingdom. It is time to reclaim your position. Nothing eliminates your feelings of inner frailty like an explosion of empowering interventions that wobble *miss-understandings* that give rise to your inner storms.

Whether it's to do with money matters, your relationships, or your bowling score, the Power of Intervention leaves you with one "*Aha!*"

moment after another, and suddenly, and suddenly, and suddenly you're able to bring anxious thinking and nervous reactions to an end.

VISIONS OF VICTORY

If only you could remember those childhood moments when you would weave enticing visions of victory and then proceed to bring them to life by taking action. For example, when you were tired of crawling and envisioned yourself walking, or you'd had it with mumbling and decided to begin talking. Oh, how confident you felt as you transformed those visions into reality.

When you live with full diligence for seeking the truth about yourself, you're on fire, and you aspire ever higher, like you did as a child. Did you know you were speaking with a 200-word vocabulary by age two, and a 10,000-word vocabulary by the age of six? (That's most of the words you still use today.) Wow!

This capacity to transform fantasy into reality is bestowed on all humanity. It's not meant to be a rarity—not now, not ever.

The process of continually weaving enticing visions and then coming up with strategies for successful action requires constant intervening. It requires being your own psychological sheepdog, herding and corralling those discouraging opinions when they begin roaming through your field of consciousness, raising havoc.

> Life's delays are never life's denials.
> However, when you delay from intervening
> On your many *miss-understandings*,
> You deny your fantasies from becoming fact.

You know when your inner court of *miss-understandings* holds a hearing on a tempting vision you're entertaining, and issues a demoralizing verdict—you feel it! Well, don't accept it! That verdict comes from a biased jury of mistaken opinions in a kangaroo court. Quickly intervene when lame excuses pop up as evidence that support such a verdict: "I object!"

The quickest way to come to your own rescue is to continually ask yourself, "How can I see this matter differently?" That one healthy question can lift your mood from helpless to promising in a moment's notice. Now, where there was weakness and waffling, there is strength and ingenuity.

You are an artist.
Your life is your work of art.
Identify with the artist within.
Resolve to solve always.
Never choose to limp when you can soar.

When you make it your mission to intervene on inner chatter when it matters, you'll soon find yourself juggling several solutions to your challenges without dropping a single one.

Right now, if you were to resolve a *miss-understanding* to claim triumph over a challenge, what vision of victory would be buzzing in your head?

- Where are you? _____
- What are you doing? _____
- Who's with you? _____
- What are you saying? _____
- What are others saying to you? _____

While answering the above questions, did any negative feelings, like frustration, envy, or resentment, pop up? That's a call for intervention! You can release this power on those negative feelings. You do it by *reinterpreting* the messages they offer.

REINTERPRETING YOUR FEELINGS

We live in a world of polarity, of contrariety, where negativity is part of the physical and emotional rainbow. Without the experience of *low* there would be no experience of *high*, hence, avoiding negativity altogether is impossible. However, you can change your attitude towards those feelings, and you can continue to "change that changed attitude" until it empowers you.

When you intervene on a negative feeling, you create a clearing for a new interpretation of that feeling, an interpretation that gives you access to a new attitude. And with that you can transform your emotional *low*s into *high*s! A simple way to begin is by asking, "What might this feeling really be trying to tell me?" Now, pause…and listen. If the answer didn't lift you high enough, ask and listen again.

Your goal of intervening on a negative feeling is to find the encouraging message behind your negative feeling. The secret to transforming something ugly into something beautiful is to repurpose the ugly so it serves you.

For example, let's look at the feeling of *frustration.*

How might you transform frustration into a tool for growth and expansion? Most folks interpret that feeling to mean, "I don't have what it takes." That mood locks their winged visions in a cage. They throw their arms up in exasperation.

Well, the truth is: you can learn from your frustration or you can mope around in resignation.

The Power of Intervention is the "key" to opening the cage door, so your vision can, once again, soar. The next time you're feeling frustrated, make that feeling your ally. What it's actually trying to tell you is this: "You are capable of succeeding, but success requires that you approach the matter differently." That message opens space for your creative nature to kick in. You begin to see options where you only saw obstacles.

Feeling frustrated is never the problem. The problem lies with your interpretation. When you feel frustrated you think the world is holding you back. Well guess what! Frustration is telling you that *you* are holding *yourself* back!

Your true artistry begins when you acknowledge your frustrations as empowering messengers, giving you the opportunity to rethink what you've previously believed.

Imagine waking up every morning looking forward to feeling frustrated because you know those moments will be opportunities to renew your sight, so you may renew your might by intervening on *miss-understandings* that have you locked up tight.

When feeling frustrated, the first thing not to do is to force an answer. Just *be* with the situation as it stands. You'll be surprised how quickly you'll open your half-shut eyes. That's when you're in for a big surprise— ideas come!

Let's look at another negative feeling—*envy.*

Envy is another empowering feeling when used resourcefully. When feeling envious, you believe you lack a quality that someone else possesses. What might happen if you intervened by directing that envy-energy toward yourself?

What if you were envious of the strengths and talents *you possess* that you've not yet accessed. If you intervene on the feeling of envy with that intention, it's not long before you'll find there is no quality of character others possess that you do not possess.

You are infinitely rich with promise.
Is that not worth envying?

I wish I could bring you back to how envious you were of your many hidden talents back when you were learning how to pour milk. An experience of euphoria washed over you as you succeeded without spilling. Then you looked around for something else to conquer. Elation came over you, again and again, as you looked forward to what was around the next corner so you could succeed at that task and get to the corner after that.

As a kid, the more envious you became of your unrealized potential, the more you reached for higher challenges, such as reading and writing and riding a bike…all in the name of understanding more of your limitless nature. In those moments you always found yourself at the edge of a new life.

Wow, the possibilities!

Let's look at one more negative feeling—*resentment.*

Resentment is a mild dislike that has intensified. You allowed the dislike to linger too long in your mind, by ruminating on it, and now it's toxic energy. However, if you direct that ruminating energy of resentment correctly, it is remarkably energizing. You find yourself ruminating on thoughts that are soothing rather than angrily steaming.

Your ability to monitor your negative feelings, so they support you, is vital to your growth. If at any time, while reading this book, you experience frustration, envy, or resentment for any reason—don't hesitate to intervene to transform that energy from toxic to helpful.

You are the only weaver sitting behind the thought-loom in your mind. Embark on your inner journey with due diligence, and your outward ambitions will become your reality. Trust this fact.

What are you weaving now? _____

What have you woven before? _____

What will you weave next? _____

A perfect, healthy practice is to make it a habit to intervene on opinions that ruin your weaving. The more you intervene, the more you remember remarkable truths about yourself that you'd long ago forgotten. And you do all this in the privacy of your own mind!

Now that you understand the Power of Intervention and the toxic nature of *overemphasizing* and *overapplying* your *miss-understandings*, let's get down to business...

chapter 3

The Supremacy of "I AM"

THE ADVANCEMENT POINT

You come to be who you are through the many "I AMs" you claim yourself to be. Those two words place you in a most intimate conversation with yourself. They are the advancement point from which your entire life proceeds. Your many "ways of being" in the world unfold from your many "I AMs"

You are "the maker" and "the made" when it comes to you. When you call forth a new "I AM," you call forth a new quality to shine through your personality. Those "I AMs" are the source of the myriad iterations found in your inner conversations that give you your responses and your actions in the world.

The more you are able to explain yourself to yourself, the more aware you are of the scores of "I AMs" that make up your identity, which explains why you behave as you do.

You cannot help but bring more of yourself into the world with every new "I AM" that you accept as true about you.

Your "I AMs" are the mainstay of your life. You cannot claim a new "I AM" without introducing a new "self" to yourself. One single shift in "I AM" immediately alters the way you occur to yourself, which immediately alters the way your world occurs for you. They show up in your relationships, your demeanor, your physiology, your inner self-talk and outer dialogue, and your behavior. You simply cannot conduct yourself in life outside of them.

For example, when you claim, "I am graceful," and identify with that claim, your world occurs for you very differently, and you show up in your world very differently than when you claim, "I am clumsy."

When a person claims, "I am clumsy," it is not an expression of his intelligence, but an expression of his confusion, coming from a *miss-understanding*. Yet that person will step into the world and prove it, so he can experience it. This happens unconsciously, but nonetheless it happens.

The problem with claiming, "I am clumsy," and proving it, is that the evidence reinforces future acts of clumsiness, and soon that person is revealing clumsiness in stereotypical fashion, tripping and spilling things constantly.

When a person claims, "I am graceful," that's an expression of his natural intelligence, and oh what a different way the world occurs for him than when he claims, "I am clumsy." Hence, he occurs in the world very differently.

It's wise to be aware of the "I AMs" you are claiming. You've got to watch out! When left unattended, the mind can go nutty with the claims it makes.

An incredible quality that comes with being a human being is the ability to claim new "I AMs" continually. At any time, you can draw a line in your mind and distinguish a new way of being by claiming a new "I AM." However, in order to do that successfully, you have to loosen your relationship with a current, opposing "I AM" that you've been committed to. We'll go into this extensively, later in the book.

SHAPING YOUR PERSONALITY

Every time you make a new claim about yourself, with a conviction to prove it, you are using the spoken word to reveal what has been concealed, and you've added another dimension to your personality.

Furthermore, every satisfying new "I AM" is a ceremony of self-perception and offers new possibilities in the face of the same old conditions. To follow through with an expression of a newly claimed "I AM" is like pulling a rabbit out of a hat! You can claim a thousand new "I AMs" and experience a thousand new states of being in the blink of an eye. There are no limits!

YOU are the sole source of your experiences of yourself. Those experiences come from you; nowhere else. How magical is that? And the more your expressions support a newly claimed "I AM," the more endurance you give that "I AM."

You think what you think, and you feel what you feel, and you act as you act, and you experience yourself as you experience yourself because of your "I AMs." The drama of being human, with innumerable "ways of being" is certainly a psychological adventure.

Your "I AMs" are the infrastructure upon which you establish everything in your life. They place you squarely in the middle of your dramas and squarely in the middle of your adventures. They offer you laughter and joy, happiness and misery.

> You bring *yourself* into your world with your "I AMs."
> You bring *your world* into the world with your "I AMs."
> Your "I AMs" set the tone for your relationship with yourself.
> Your "I AMs" set the tone for your relationships with everyone.
> Your "I AMs" are your messengers to the world.
> Your "I AMs" announce you to your world.

Your world is an omnipresent mirror, ever reflecting back, with impeccable precision, what you outwardly project. If you're to change the world in which you dwell, first you must change the "I AMs" that dwell in you.

You cannot say, "I AM," without referring to yourself in the first person, present tense. That's as intimate as you can get. Your "I AMs" shape your psychology, they are the bedrock of your personality, they give you your unique model of reality. That's why claiming new "I AMs" can feel risky!

BORN AGAIN

You experience a shift in consciousness when you claim a new "I AM" and mean it. That shift offers you a new experience of "being" that was not available before. That's what it is to have a *born again* experience. You've given yourself over to a new identity, which takes you deeper into the many dimensions of being a human being.

Born again experiences require an openness to newness. Children just love being *born again*, and *again*, and *again*; they love the breakthrough adventure that comes with claiming unfamiliar territory. Those "I AM" moments set them free to express themselves, fresh and new, repeatedly. That's how they grow. That's how *you* grew.

Think about it: you can claim an "I AM" today, become thoroughly acquainted with that "I AM" tomorrow, and then acquaint yourself with a *new* "I AM" the next day! How can your life possibly be boring! Nothing feels more satisfying than your wizardry when you break through to a new "way of being."

> Your experience of life is a delicious upward flight,
> Ever ascending higher when you get your "I AMs" right.

Read here

When a tiny tot claims (unconsciously), "I am a walker," and identifies with that claim, they do whatever has to be done to stand up and walk, including pulling themselves up by the dog's tail if need be. And once they're on the move, there's no stopping them. They walk into one new reality after another with newly claimed "I AMs" leading the way, each inspiring them to make another claim that brings forth yet another possibility.

"I'm going to be a doctor…. No, wait…I'm going to be a rodeo bull rider…. No, no, I know…. I'm going to be an astronaut!" Do you know why children love to tell you what they're going to be when they grow up? They love expressing that which was inexpressible just a moment ago.

Are you still like that ambitious tiny tot you once were? There is a resourceful part of you that is always waiting to express more of the inexpressible you. That is the "hope of glory" found in all children. It is the "hope of glory" to which all adults yearn to return. So many "I AMs" to become familiar with.

Do you know why growth feels so painful? It's because we learn to cling to what's predictable.

> With change comes unpredictability.
> With unpredictability comes possibility.
> With possibility comes the unthinkable.
> The next thing you know you're expressing the inexpressible.
> The quest for grander expansion is inward.
> The pursuit of fuller expression is outward.
> Don't be shy about expressing yourself anew.
> For the sake of your evolution it's what you have to do.

HIGH-FLYING BUTTERFLIES

Do you know the difference between a crawling caterpillar that *dies crawling,* and a crawling caterpillar that *transforms into a high-flying butterfly?* The former looks up at the sky, *wishing* it could fly, but is always conscious of itself as a *crawling caterpillar.* The latter looks up at the sky, claiming it can fly, and is conscious of itself flying even while it's still crawling. Bingo!

If you're to fly high, you must be conscious of flying high and draw no boundaries when it's time to claim your wings. Prescriptions for higher living are of little value until we stop living like the caterpillar that's *wishing* and *hoping* but stuck in "I AMs" that have us crawling.

There's not an "I AM" in your personality that has a lifetime guarantee, unless *you* guarantee it.

If you're dissatisfied with the results your "I AMs" are giving you—you can replace them. Doing that requires being *unreasonable,* which requires applying extra elbow grease by intervening on your usual ways of reasoning.

The first step to making a change in the "I AMs" that make up your identity is being awake to the fact that a change is needed. The next step is to claim and identify with a new "I AM" that supports the way you want to be. This often requires letting go of familiar *miss-understandings* that insist you are who you are, and there's nothing you can do about it. This is when you have to step beyond what your reasoning mind is telling you.

Unreasonableness is your Get Out of Jail Free card. Your jail is your familiar comfort zone, where your many self-limiting "I AMs" dwell. The bars of your jail are your many reasonable explanations and rationalizations that keep those "I AMs" thriving.

Nothing is a bigger stumbling block to stepping beyond your comfort zone than the statement, "This is just the way I am." If you ever hear yourself saying that, honor yourself by intervening, and be a pouncing tiger about it. Don't hesitate.

Your hot point of power is always "right now." Your opportunity to stop misbegotten "I AMs" from holding a lifelong position in your belief system, is right now.

When intervening, merely saying, "I will be…" won't cut it. That's the attitude of a jumping flea. It's a prediction about tomorrow, but tomorrow never comes.

The real problem with saying, "I will be…" is that you're actually saying, "I am *not* that right now," hence, you are granting power to the "*not.*" Your comfort zone becomes your *dead zone* when you're stuck those *nots.* Where's the juice? Where's the feeling of aliveness? Where's the growth?

You're only stuck in your *dead zone* when you say, "This is just the way I am," and refuse to budge from that position. With that one declarative statement you immediately come up with a dozen *reasonable* justifications, which guarantees stagnation.

If you intend to undergo your own personal metamorphosis from a caterpillar to a butterfly, you must be uncooperative with your reasoning mind about how high you can fly. Envision success no matter what the mess!

> To those who believe they are but tiny pebbles
> At the bottom of the mountain, look again.
> The truth be told: you are the entire mountain.

Does the above statement seem unreasonable to you? Be prepared to betray any lingering thoughts that make you doubt you are the entire mountain. That kind of doubting is an act of betrayal against yourself. Intervene immediately on all such self-doubting opinions. Never allow your well-organized, reasonable ways of thinking to convince you that you are but a tiny pebble at the base of the mountain. Dare to intervene, and before you know it you'll begin experiencing your *miss-understandings* as mere whimpering whispers.

YOU WOULDN'T IF YOU COULDN'T

Here is timely fact, worthy of your attention: *You would not desire to be a specific "I AM" if you could not be that "I AM."* Are you willing to accept that as true? So then, what's to stop you from lifting those thousands of constraints you've imposed upon yourself?

Life never constrains you.
If you're feeling constrained,
You are constraining yourself.
Seeing yourself correctly removes the shackles
You've strapped around your ankles.
When you are shackle-free
You advance with relaxed efficiency.
Beneficence waits.
Dare to roam in your imagination.
Dare to come to stately opinions of yourself.

Nothing can stop you, other than you, from building stately mansions in which to live your life. No more straw huts for you. The blessing of being a human being is your ability to change an "I AM" in mid-stream. It's a great relief to know you can claim a new "I AM" and confirm a new identity if you don't like who you've assumed yourself to be. Do you agree?

When I was a kid, I loved imitating Jerry Lewis, the famous comedian. My grandfather would laugh and say, "Bobby, you're funny." I jumped on that comment immediately, and exclaimed with conviction, "I *am* funny!" I seized my hot point of power and delighted in saying funny things. It wasn't long before "being funny" became part of my identity. Even today, most folks think I am funny…I think?

In my early teens I made another claim: "I am a troublemaker." I didn't *consciously* claim it, but I would start trouble at the drop of a hat, so I must have done so unconsciously. I remember when I renounced that claim for something better. I'd gotten in trouble in high school for being rude to the principal. My guidance counselor told me if I intended to go to college, I'd better *stop* being a troublemaker. She suggested I become a trouble-solver instead. I wasn't aware you could do that. It took some effort, but I did it.

Whenever you knock on the door of a new "I AM," and knock with confidence, practical ways to assume that identity will come. That's when it's time to step up and take action.

It's time to grab a pen again.
Let's do a self-awareness exercise.
Are you ready?
Be generous when you write.

SELF-AWARENESS EXERCISE

1. If I were *unreasonable* with my aims and aspirations, what "I AM" would I claim?

   _____

2. If I felt certain my efforts would be effective, what action would I take?

   _____

3. Now go to a mirror and look at yourself. What do you see behind those eyes looking back at you? (Breathe deeply and listen. Can you hear the chains unshackling?)

   _____

One more question:

4. If I were free of the beehive of excuses buzzing in my head, what *other* "I AM" would I enjoy claiming?

   _____

(You did the exercise, right?)

The next time you're feeling stuck, and you assume something's *wrong* with you, take time to remind yourself, "Yes, there's something *wrong*, but it's not with *me*. What's *wrong* are the restraints I'm imposing on myself by believing that foolish assumption." Now what "I AM" might you claim?

THIEVES!

Your self-imposed restraints are thieves in the night, stealing your creativity. Your innovative nature is tightly sealed until you reveal and dismiss such restraints. Grant yourself permission to do that. The more you engage in the practice of dealing with these thieves, the more inspired you are to call a bluff on any "I AMs" that casts you in a spell of perplexity.

Indeed, you live in a world of contradiction where both crawling caterpillars and high-flying butterflies exist. You cannot escape that. However, when you are faced with a contradiction that gives you the option of crawling or flying, support the idea of flying. Oh, what a dreadful price you pay when you refuse to play the game of life as it is meant to be played.

Put down those poison darts you constantly toss at your heart when you fail at something new. Be unflinching when it's time to take action to reach your unique style of excellence. Accept your limitlessness as fact, and the darts you fling will lose their sting. Better yet, you'll stop flinging darts.

Ponder this chapter before moving on. Allow its rescuing messages to flash like flames across the open sky of your mind. Soon, you are going to learn how to productively package your dynamic "I AMs" by putting together a dynamic *To-Be* list. That's coming up in Chapter 9.

Let's linger for a moment.

Enjoy the receptive state you now find yourself in.

Can you feel it?

Great!

What better time than now to introduce you to something remarkable...

chapter 4

The Ultimate Understanding

LISTEN INTENTLY

There is a voice speaking from deep within, offering you precious counseling. It is urging you to *no longer* keep *who you are* a secret from yourself. To be loyal to that voice is to be true to your original nature. That voice is the "Maestro," the boundless, interminable you, which will be unveiled, completely, in Chapter 18.

Until you uncover the basic structure of your *being*, and become aware of yourself as a possibility for infinite possibilities—most of your ebullient, splendorous entirety will slip by, unnoticed.

In the soulful poem, *A Lost Chord*, by Adelaide Anne Procter,[3] she speaks of an organ player who was feeling weary as she played on and on. Then she happened upon one marvelous chord of exquisite harmony. The chord transformed her mood magnificently. It quieted all her pain and sorrow. And after having played that chord, she sought and sought, but sought in vain to find that chord again.

The Ultimate Understanding (UU) empowers you to break free from any complications that stop you from experiencing your own exquisite lost chord. When you experience the UU, you are like a wondrous organ, tuned in the perfect key. Your life is in flow and you take on a euphoric glow. A phenomenal feeling of balance and unity comes over you, and your face lights up with a thousand smiles as you rise above all discordance.

Without further ado, I give you the diamond of truth that offers you captaincy of your destiny so that you may experience your own *lost chord*. It is written in first person, present tense because it is meant to be taken personally.

THE ULTIMATE UNDERSTANDING

I am a rich and majestic child of infinite intelligence.
I am marvelously made.
I am here to reveal, feel, and share
all that is good and beautiful about me.

The UU is inviting you to experience yourself accurately. To truly embrace the UU is to reflect on yourself at a depth far beyond cerebral conceptualization. It opens you to a super intelligence that exists in each of us, which has you look at yourself very differently.

Your origin is independent of your ancestry. You are a being of 24-karat quality, a splendid part of the entire cosmic symphony. Your willingness to entertain this truth places you in an alert state of consciousness that far transcends your conditioned ways of thinking about yourself.

As you come to know what is already true about you, of which your surface mind is currently unaware, and to be in the face of it without flinching, you evolve with new expressions that far transcend daily distractions and pointless activity.

TRULY LIVING FOR YOURSELF

To embrace the UU as "your truth" requires that you let it be your launching pad for ever higher aims and expressions of yourself. Only then can you begin truly living for yourself, which is when you place yourself in an optimal mood of thanksgiving. Consequently, your interactions with your world are warm and engaging. And the better it gets for you, the better it gets for everyone in your world.

Let's now say the UU aloud together. Chopin chose only the *right notes* to attain a musical revolution of grace and beauty. Allow the UU to strike those *right notes* with your tonality, so you may begin your own emotional revelation of elegant artistry.

Absorb every word, with all its nuances. Allow what you are saying to overwhelm any insecurities you may be entertaining.

Relax.
Breathe in slowly through your nose.
Hold your breath for the count of four.
Now release your breath slowly through your mouth and speak purposefully.

I am a rich and majestic child of infinite intelligence.
I am marvelously made.
I am here to reveal, feel, and share
all that is good and beautiful about me.

The UU is right-reality. It's life-giving. It creates space for other stars of truth to burn zealously in your consciousness. Imagine the spirit of the UU being the nucleus of your state of being. What could be more refreshing?

Does good fortune only select but a few to experience the UU? Nay, nay! Good fortune selects anyone who elects to be selected to experience the benefits the UU offers.

An inner chime is ringing.
Listen! You are being called.
Life is abundance overflowing.
You are abundance overflowing.
You are a majestic child of the infinite.
You are marvelously made.
You are a treasure trove of good and beautiful potential.

The possibilities that *come* with the truth of your infinite nature are infinite. That's the truth, and the truth is the truth with nothing to explain. Deliverance dawns when you choose what's true over your *miss-understandings*.

The UU reveals *who* you are, *what* you are, and *why* you are here, which adds a revolution of "creative seasoning" to your personality. It creates a clearing for you to share all that is good and beautiful about yourself in 1,001 ways, with everyone, every day. Furthermore, it creates innumerable opportunities for you to experience how good and beautiful everyone else can be. As you can see, there is nothing "holier-than-thou" about the UU.

Nothing can lure you from your natural stream of wondrous expressions but your pre-programmed, patterned ways of thinking. Therefore, I must caution you…

BE NOT LIKE NAAMAN

Naaman was the commander of the King of Aram's army. A chivalrous, highly respected warrior was he, despite suffering with leprosy. One day, he went to the prophet Elisha for healing advice. He told him to wash seven times in the Jordan River.

The prophet's simple instructions angered Naaman. He had expected more pomp and circumstance in the healing of his affliction. After all, he was the commander of a great army! Anyone could do what Elisha advised. There had to be more to it than that.

Naaman stormed away. However, eventually he humbled himself and performed the act Elisha advised. He washed seven times in the river and was healed.[4]

Be *not* like Naaman. *Don't* require a big hullabaloo to cleanse your mind of bewildering disillusionment that prevents you from accepting the Ultimate Understanding. Perhaps turning from the darkness of your *miss-understandings,* so you may bathe in the light of the UU, will take more than one washing of the mind. Perhaps you'll need to wash seven times or 77 times. So be it.

> Let there be light.
> It requires no might.
> Delusion begets confusion.
> Awareness rids delusion.

There is no better way to begin a mystical love affair with yourself than to embrace the UU. It will have you experiencing yourself in many new ways in your day. No two people come to know the UU in the same way.

Prepare to say the UU again, but this time speak it with the intention of observing any opposing point of view that your usual way of thinking imposes on you. Don't fight it, just observe.

Ready?

Try singing the words from your heart, so you feel its rapture.

> *I am a rich and majestic child of infinite intelligence.*
> *I am marvelously made.*
> *I am here to reveal, feel, and share*
> *all that is good and beautiful about me.*

Did you hear any thought-voice mocking you while speaking the UU? The only dividing line between you and the UU are lines drawn in your mind by your *miss-understandings*. It's time for you to step over those lines. Again, you would not be reading this book if it wasn't your time.

JOAN

Joan has a beautiful backyard filled with flowers and hummingbirds. She loves her hummingbird friends, they bring her great pleasure. Ellen, Joan's favorite hummingbird, lands on her shoulder whenever she wears her pink cotton sweater. Joan will tell you that these marvelous creatures are indisputable evidence of infinite intelligence expressing itself in the world.

"How could they be anything less?" she comments. "They fly so delicately!"

By viewing her colorful backyard friends this way, Joan has stepped over the line in her own mind by embracing the UU for herself. Perhaps her backyard friends cannot lend their marvelous wings to help her fly as nimbly as they do, but she'll eagerly tell you that Ellen has nudged her awake to her own unique wings.

Joan just completed a book of beautiful poems, a project she'd been working on for years. And now she's flying even higher still—the book was just picked up by a publishing company.

What dream might you bring to reality if you accepted the UU as a foundational part of what you are? The possibilities are staggering, aren't they?

Imagine walking down the street, recognizing everyone you meet as a rich and majestic child of infinite intelligence. Imagine speaking with friends with the same attitude that Joan has for her hummingbird friends. When you make the slightest effort to recognize the UU in others—as Joan does with Ellen—you cannot help but feel that way about yourself.

> What thou *see-eth*, thou *be-eth*.
> The more you see others through the eyes of the UU,
> the more you see *yourself* through the eyes of the UU.
> It's unavoidable.

Thinking of yourself as anything less than the UU would be like a giant oak tree observing a single leaf on one of its branches and saying, "That's all there is of me."

> Oh, glory be!
> There's so much more to you.
> You'll see!
> Express even a little wish to leave the lower,
> And the higher will rush to you.

Are you familiar with Psalm 121? "I will lift up mine eyes unto the hills, from whence cometh my help"?[5] Lift your eyes to the UU, and with earnest effort, your *miss-understandings* clear themselves so you can reveal yourself.

I suggest you take a pleasant stroll today and keep a lookout for others who have lifted their eyes. They are the peaceful ones with warm smiles on their faces. Seek to understand what they understand about themselves. You'll find that they accept the UU in their own exclusive way.

OPEN THE GATE

If you're feeling uncertain about what you are stating, don't be afraid to be uncertain. Uncertainty, when patiently withstood, leads to certainty. Once you get into this, you'll be as eager as a young colt yearning to run free as it waits for the ranch hand to open the gate.

The difference between you and the young colt is that you are also the ranch hand, and the field in which you yearn to freely run is your own field of consciousness.

Are you ready to claim the UU one last time before leaving this chapter? Make it your intention to monopolize your attention by *feeeeling* the truth of what you are speaking. If you sow your attention sparingly, you reap sparingly. If you sow your attention bountifully, you reap bountifully.

Ok, let's speak it together.

> *I am a rich and majestic child of infinite intelligence.*
> *I am marvelously made.*
> *I am here to reveal, feel, and share*
> *all that is good and beautiful about me.*

The UU, spoken several times daily, will replenish and refresh your stream of thoughts like a mountain stream replenishes and refreshes a mighty river. That's a spiritual fact.

THEY STAND AS ONE

Although the UU can be broken into three parts, they stand as one. However, if one part delightfully pokes at your heart, embrace it. The more you embrace that one part of the UU, the more comfortable you'll become with the whole. In other words, if you pledge to be true to any one of the three parts of the UU, with all that you say and do, all three will be as loyal to you as are the roots that carry sustenance to the budding flowers of a rosebush.

In the following three chapters we will examine the UU from the perspective of *who* you are, *what* you are, and *why* you are here. This will give you a better grasp of the UU in its entirety.

Prepare to venture forth valorously as you begin saying goodbye to the old and welcoming the new…

chapter 5

A Rich and Majestic Child

COMING TO KNOW THE WHO OF YOU

The first part of the Ultimate Understanding opens your heart to a monumental truth: you are a rich and majestic child of infinite intelligence. Understanding this requires understanding yourself as "the source" of your wondrous expressions.

When you ask yourself, "Who am I?" your beliefs are quick to supply answers, and those answers have become *law* in your life. There is within you amazing wisdom and intelligence far surpassing your patterned ways of thinking. That's what we are now looking at.

Let's speak this first part of the UU together.

Though I am not with you physically, surely by now our minds are mingling. Use your richest, fullest vocal expression. Hold nothing back. Claim it as though it is something vitally important to remember.

It is!

I am a rich and majestic child of infinite intelligence.
This is who I am.
I am a rich and majestic child of infinite intelligence.

Convictions are born when your claims are distinct. Hence, I've added *"This is who I am"* to jog your memory to what you'd long ago forgotten about yourself.

Understanding yourself as a child of infinite intelligence is *not* about commanding the universe; it's about recognizing your origin as a mystery. As advanced as our anthropology and archaeology may be, our origin still lies in secrecy. Have you heard the Bible verse, "I am the vine, ye are the branches?"[6] Imagine this first line of the UU as the vine. With that in mind, what "I AMs" might you branch off from it?

> Your children are not your children.
> They are the sons and daughters of Life's longing for itself.
> They come through you but not from you,
> And though they are with you, yet they belong not to you.
>
> —Kahlil Gibran[7]

Gibran was not referring to the child found in your genealogical chart, but rather, he was describing the child that has been around for eternity. Are you not one of the children of whom Gibran was speaking?

Sound intriguing?

Listen to the oracle within. It is speaking to you: "It is sad that you react to the world like it's a dangerous jungle, my child. Look deeper into yourself and understand from whence you really come. Otherwise, you destroy your highest purpose, your greatest growth, and your grandest joy. You are an unfailing source of creative energy, but it's simply *not* possible to make vital changes in your life without first making vital changes in your self-understanding."

Did you hear the message? A right search into your origin begins with realizing you're not sure what to expect, and yet anticipating that your discovery is extraordinary.

IT'S PRACTICAL AND SPIRITUAL

When your identity includes being a rich and majestic child of infinite intelligence, you find yourself transforming your daily, practical involvements into spiritual experiences. You do that by extracting meaning from these experiences that advance and enhance your life.

Your life is always meant to be a spiritual and practical act of harmony. Hence, whenever something is truly spiritual it is also practical and useable. Sort of like learning to dance. The spirituality of dancing is found in the rhythm, and the practicality is found in hours of practice, perfecting your dance steps. Combine the two, and now you have something! You're a fabulous dancer and you can feel it!

In this state of mind, your life becomes a commitment to unending spiritual promises in which you engage in life, in hands-on ways, that have you living creatively, reverently, and productively all at the same time. In such moments, you commission the exact right measure of activity even while achieving your most mundane daily tasks.

So, what does it mean to be a rich and majestic child of infinite intelligence? It means being your own unique self, which can be challenging when living in a community that insists you be who "they" want you to be.

The most powerful driving force in the human psyche is to live according to *who* you consider yourself to be. If you come upon anyone who insists you are *less* than a rich and majestic child, understand that their opinion is merely a limit in *their* perception. It is your responsibility to choose to be on your side, always. No need to argue with them, but certainly do not agree.

As a rich and majestic child of infinite intelligence, you have the power to oust any "I AM" that's causing you problems. Be ye a rich man, poor man, beggar man, or thief, that is entirely up to you. You have the capacity to be rich in all dimensions of life: rich with love, rich with gentility, rich with compassion, and rich materially. If any of these feel foreign to you, it's because you're still identifying with a *miss-understanding* that has you feeling like a "poor man" in some way.

Your "I AMs" may be powerful forces in your identity, but they are not immutable. One slight turn of your mental rudder—one newly introduced "I AM," if claimed with conviction, can set you in an entirely new direction. We'll deal with all of this later.

An interesting phenomenon is that when you genuinely embody this first part of the UU, you feel no need to prove it, and furthermore, you leave space for everyone else to feel that way about themselves, too. And coincidentally, the more you grant others the freedom to feel that way, the more freedom you grant yourself.

THE GREATER HE

The Bible verse "Greater is he that is in you than he that is in the world"[8] has always intrigued me. Could it be, the "greater he" within you and me is the rich and majestic child of infinite intelligence? Could it also be, the "lesser he" within you is the *intruder*, who insists you're far less than that?

A perfect way to feel empowered is to remind yourself a dozen times daily that you've always been and always will be a rich and majestic child of infinite intelligence, and that *this* is the "greater he" that is in you. When this fact settles in, it sheds light on those many shadows of confusion that your *miss-understandings* have cast over the truth about you.

At times, especially when I face a difficulty, I find it reassuring to remind myself, "This difficulty is outmatched by the *greater me*." Then I claim this first part of the UU to remind myself of my original heritage. Let's claim it again, and this time in a kingly fashion.

> *I am a rich and majestic child of infinite intelligence.*
> *This is who I am.*
> *I am a rich and majestic child of infinite intelligence.*

I enjoy decreeing this part of the UU to remind myself continually that *I am the conceiver* of who I claim myself to be. I also enjoy decreeing this part of the UU to remind myself that *I am also the conception.* That means I inevitably experience what I conceive. In such moments it is clear to me that this life is meant to be a pleasant and joyful journey.

> You are the conceiver.
> You are the conception.
> *Who* next will you conceive yourself to be?
>
> Your next "I AM" becomes your new concept of yourself.
> Your new concept becomes your next expression.
> This expression becomes your new experience of yourself.
>
> Voilà! It is done.

As the conceiver, you recognize there is always a new conception of yourself waiting to manifest. In that high state of awareness, you are free of any internal yammering that insists that your talents are scanty. That's when even the slightest urge to claim a new "I AM" can prove to be the perfect decision. When you're touched like that, breathtaking ideas percolate through you.

There is something appealing and refreshing about people who tune in to their many talents and strengths. That's because when they tune in, they tune *out* their mechanical reactions, which creates space for innovative and interesting conversations.

Have you heard the story of the truck wedged under a bridge in a busy city? Three engineers stood scratching their heads, trying to come up with a feasible and reasonable plan to jack up the bridge so the truck could pass through. A young schoolboy passing by asked, "Why don't you let the air out of the tires?" This story points to a groundbreaking question: How often are we so blinded by our mental programming that we cannot see how simple it can be to free ourselves from misconceptions of inadequacy?

The next time you're feeling stuck, like a truck wedged under a bridge, take a moment to relax and remind yourself of your origin. If you do this earnestly, your attitude will shift to eager expectancy as you seek an answer to your dilemma. First will come mental calmness, then confident curiosity, and then you will be struck with an intuitive insight. This insight offers you a truth that lets the air out of the tires of that "feeling of *stuckness.*"

IT'S FOR ALL SEASONS

Being a rich and majestic child of infinite intelligence is a powerful truth to be experienced in every season of your life. Be it spring, summer, fall, or winter—when you understand yourself that way, a gratifying feeling supports you on even the coldest day.

Are you ready to affirm this part of the UU one more time before leaving the chapter? Be completely present with yourself as you make the claim. Release the words fully into your consciousness.

Become a source of incalculable confidence as you say:

> *I am a rich and majestic child of infinite intelligence.*
> *This is who I am.*
> *I am a rich and majestic child of infinite intelligence.*

Has claiming this part of the UU brought anything to mind about yourself that you didn't realize you already knew? Bask in that feeling for a moment, no matter how slight the glimpse of it may be. Did you experience a warm glow while making this claim? Great, it's beginning to settle in.

Now that you know *who* you truly are, let's move on to the second part of the UU...

chapter 6

Marvelously Made

COMING TO KNOW *WHAT* YOU TRULY ARE

It takes courage to lean on nothing outside of yourself when it comes to taking a stand about *what* it means to be a human being. However, there is a gift that comes with that kind of courage—exposure to an inner compass that directs you toward grander expressions of even your simplest leanings.

First you came into the world, then you came to be who you are today in the world. When you submit to the leanings of your authentic *beingness*, even your simplest responses to life show up in unpredictable ways that have satisfying consequences. That's when humanity's majesty shines through brightly.

Take a moment to relish what you're contemplating right now. To be marvelously praised by yourself is to be marvelously raised by yourself. If you're to have any chance of probing into the depths of your marvelously made nature, you've got to turn up the heat on your curiosity.

You are investigating yourself in a way that offers a whole new design for what it is to be a human being. One of the aims of this part of the UU is to startle you. Otherwise, your mechanical mind will continue to churn out those same thoughts today about you that it churned out yesterday.

You are a being with remarkable capacities. However, to claim you are *marvelously made* can feel a bit overboard. Why? Those *miss-understandings* you came to years ago refuse to let go.

Are you ready to claim the second part of the Ultimate Understanding? Let's speak the words together in an inviting manner. Perhaps you add a little dazzle by speaking the words with a foreign accent, so it "pops" for you.

> Breathe in.
> Hold your breath to the count of four.
> Breathe out slowly.
> Relax.
> Are you ready?
> Drum roll, please!

I am marvelously made.
This is what I am.
I am marvelously made.

What opinion might you hold of yourself that needs correction so you can live by the truth of your marvelously made nature? Just be with that query for a moment.

Questions like the above can help jog you out of your customary line of reasoning. When the mind is dazed by unusual questions it's not used to, the chatter slows. This creates space for you to re-evaluate yourself from a new perspective. That's when insights and breakthroughs happen.

When you first explore yourself beyond your accustomed reasoning, the experience may be like dropping a rock onto dry sand and expecting a splash—you'll feel disappointed. But if you sustain your inquiry, and are not greedy for a quick answer, you'll find yourself stepping beyond your habitual ways of seeing things. That's when you're able to examine and express more of your intelligence and less of your programmed nescience.

René Descartes' philosophy fits perfectly with what we're exploring: "I think, therefore I am." When you genuinely *think* you are marvelously made, you find it easier to demonstrate the qualities that come with that opinion, and soon you find "you are that."

In the grandest of times, everyone dances to their own unique drumbeat with dignity and gentility. I urge you never to muffle the marvelous drumbeat to which you came to dance, and never, never to muffle your words when you say to yourself, "I am marvelously made."

Our customary way of speaking of ourselves leaves out so much of the truth. Let's look at something you've always known about yourself at some level, but rarely have been able to find words to describe.

A QUICKENING

Martha Graham, an influential choreographer of modern dance, whose works help reveal the mystery of the inner being, does a wonderful job of describing the lifeforce of humanity—that energy which is always prompting you to express your marvelously made nature.

> There is a vitality, a life force, an energy, a quickening, that is
> translated through you into action, and because there is only one of
> you in all of time, this expression is unique. And if you block it,
> it will never exist through any other medium, and be lost.
>
> —Martha Graham to Agnes De Mille[9]

When you give permission for this *quickening* to translate through you—you experience an arousal of ardor that inspires you to be yourself and no one else but yourself. You're walking on sacred ground. That's when your marvelously made nature manifests into the light of day.

Martha Graham also mentions there is only one of you in all of time, and your expressions of your marvelous qualities are unique to you. That quickening that stirs within you is your capacity to demonstrate the distinctive rhythm of *your* drumbeat.

Imagine what your life would be like if you walked through your day aware of your quickening wanting to express in marvelous ways. How might you allow that life-force energy to translate through you? Right there, you'll find what you dream of experiencing—the indescribable you!

Is it possible your quickening has, already at times, translated through you into action? Are you raising your eyebrows, wondering when? Turn away from what you presently remember, and allow your mind to recall a scene, a moment in your past where you felt truly comfortable with yourself as you danced or told an arousing story or wrote a poem. It could have been a childhood expression, or something in the past few years, that you'd forgotten all about.

Let no one tell you that your quickening is a myth. Accept the truth, allow your curiosity to arouse earnest interest that prompts the question, "What's next for me?"

A wild lion was captured and placed in a zoo with other lions that had been captured years ago. When the newcomer spoke of the quickening that stirred within him, the others laughed. A few nights later, the pride gathered together to sing songs about a land without fences where one roams and freely expresses his *lionly* prowess.

It wasn't but a day later that the newcomer found an opportunity to jump the fence, and so returned to that land that the other lions only sang about. Your opportunity is coming to jump any fence you've placed in front of you, any limiting belief that keeps you locked in your confining comfort zone, any assumption that stops you from freely expressing your prowess.

Bask in the recuperative feeling that comes with acknowledging the fact that if you block your unique expression, it will never exist through any other medium, and will be lost forever…and then say, "If it is to be, it is up to me."

When you have faith in yourself, and you call upon your quickening with the intention of experiencing breathtaking expressions of your marvelously made nature—even if life sends a stormy wind to batter you about, you'll find yourself standing sturdy, never losing sight of what feels right for you.

What if you saw a giant pine tree producing big, red, juicy apples? You'd find that unimaginably unpredictable, wouldn't you? Well, perhaps such miracles are *impossible* for a pine tree, but not for you! You'll find your truest pleasure lies in probing the depths and the heights of your myriad possibilities of expression.

Okay then, let's speak this part of the UU again, and this time with a full intention of owning it.

I am marvelously made.
This is what I am.
I am marvelously made.

With this one ray of truth you can begin breaking through years of dark *miss-understandings*. Surrender any notion you're entertaining that this has to be difficult to grasp.

Speaking of marvelously made, what about your body? Let's take a look.

YOUR MARVELOUS BOD

Have you ever thought about the fact that there is not a cell in your body that tears that does not know how to repair itself? Every cell naturally seeks perfection, which is apparent when you cut your finger. Each cell immediately kicks into action, and does an incredible job, swiftly healing. How's that for marvelously made? Is this not technology at its highest design?

And what about your immune system? Your body comes fully equipped with an exquisite chemistry kit, with every muscle, bone, and organ having access to it. Furthermore, the 78 organs of your body are not only in tune with one another but are also completely in tune with the infinite intelligence of nature's biological system. This enables your entire anatomy—cardiovascular, respiratory, and digestive systems—to work together with impeccable precision. All of that, right there, is light years ahead of anything modern science can comprehend.

Furthermore, your body can discriminate with remarkable precision between the food you ingest that needs assimilating so you can grow swift and strong, and the food you ingest that needs eliminating so you can remain healthy. How can you be anything but *marvelously made* when your body is so "up to speed?"

Would it be outrageous to consider your body your temple? If you are a rich and majestic child of infinite intelligence, what could be more fitting?

Know ye not that ye are the temple of God…?

1 Corinthians 3:16 (KJV)[10]

Just flirting with the idea that your body is a living, breathing temple in which you get to dwell, can mark the beginning of a new age of thinking. You are *marvelously* made, not miserably made. Within you is a constant nudging, reminding you of that. The more you notice that nudging, and act on it, the easier it is to notice it again.

In that state of mind, do you know what may happen the next time you visit a friend?

You: Knock, knock
Friend: "Who's there?"
You: Never again do you answer, "It's *just* me," and because you are fully aware that "just me" does yourself a grave injustice.

Feeling marvelously made has yet another perk that comes with it. That feeling helps you develop a healthy relationship with your defeats.

FAILURES ARE FUNCTIONS OF SUPPORT

Whenever you succeed at something new, that's not the end of your challenges. Your new successes inevitably come with new challenges that will certainly cause you to trip and fall once again. However, when you experience yourself as marvelously made, you stop looking at your failures as something to make excuses about, but rather as "functions of support."

Failure-free is something we'll never be, however, when you see your failures as revolutionary moments, offering you opportunities to experience more of all your marvelous faculties—your failures become your teachers, helping you learn what you need to know in order to grow. How dry and boring life would be without them!

There's only one way to avoid failing, and that's "to be idle." Unfortunately though, to be idle is to be a stranger to learning, and to be a stranger to learning is to suffocate your quickening. I've found that the more I see my failures as opportunities, and seize the moment to access more of my potential—that's when I experience my quickening translating into action.

Everything I'm sharing here applies to everyone, everywhere. Every member of the human family contains all the marvelous qualities of humanity. To feel marvelously made is never about vain theatrics. In fact, it's the quite the opposite. You take delight in letting go of any theatrical way that you've been conducting your life. And that's because you are far more interested in *expressing* yourself in order to grow, than trying to *impress* the world in order to look good. And furthermore, you are far more interested in granting everyone else that same privilege.

ONE RAY

Every ray of the sun is an expression of the attributes of light and warmth found in the entirety of the sun. Every member of the human family is meant to be a warm and inviting expression of the entirety of humanity. Let's think this through. Let's look at you.

Your body is your temple.
Your resilience is immeasurable.
Your potential is indescribable.
Your quickening is waiting for your translation.
Your opportunities to translate it are boundless.

Are you ready to do yourself a favor and trust that you *are* marvelously made? When you do yourself that favor, you do the whole human family a favor. That's because when you are conscious of yourself that way, you contribute to all of humanity feeling that way.

Every child yearns to live joyfully on the open plains of life.
Every child yearns to express unabashedly.
Every child has the capacity to explore unfathomable realities.
Every child has the capacity to experience quickenings.
Every adult is a child inside.

Experiencing yourself as a marvelously made child of infinite intelligence requires giving yourself over to that exuberant child, once again. That's when your actions are natural, and you realize the best of you is always yet to come.

Tick-tock, tick-tock. Perfect timing. Let's claim this part of the UU a third time.

Carefully articulate every syllable as you release confidence into your tone of voice. Don't forget to give real punch to the statement, "This is *what* I am." There's an unwavering spirit of optimism that overcomes you when you *feeeel* what you're saying. Let it overcome you!

I am marvelously made.
This is what I am.
I am marvelously made.

What might you do today to prove to yourself that you are marvelously made? Have you ever imagined trying something daring and new, only to have that vision quickly fade? Do you know why that vision couldn't gain a stronghold in your mind? It's because you were not willing to die in order to feel fully alive.

DYING TO FEEL ALIVE

It's a mistake to think you can accomplish a goal that is daring and new while living with "I AM" that is limiting you. It seems the only way to create space for "the new" to sprout through is the death of the old.

Children continuously take on new challenges by allowing old "I AMs" to die. And the great gain they get is *growth*. They intuitively know that they must die of "being an infant that crawls and mumbles" in order to become a "tot who learns to walk and talk." If you could only remember the many "I AMs" you allowed to die so you could mature and grow.

> Man is immortal; therefore he must die endlessly.
> For life is a creative idea; it can only find itself in changing forms.
>
> —Rabindranath Tagore[11]

Perhaps you've not thought of it this way, but you've proven your immortality, as a marvelously made being, by dying 1,000 deaths, as you advanced from age two to four to seven to nine to 12 to 15 to 22. This kind of dying had you feel like you were thriving. You dropped one identity to take on another, so you might continually express and experience yourself differently.

What could be more rejuvenating than endlessly dying, with the intention of resurrecting new "I AMs" that support your visions of exciting, new achievements? Every time you die in that fashion, you awaken a little more of what has always been half-asleep in you. This may sound strange, but it's true! Ignorance is *not* bliss when it comes to understanding this. When we get to the Maestro Monologue (Chapter 24), you'll learn precisely how to handle this.

Too long have you looked *outside* of yourself, hoping to find that special something to light you up with creative passion. Looking outside is a distraction. What you seek is within reach, but only if you *reach within*.

> It is not far, it is within reach,
> Perhaps you have been on it since you were born and did not know.
>
> —Walt Whitman[12]

The worst thing you can do for yourself is remain ignorant of the truth about yourself. Out of your ignorance can grow what you want to know. Dare to look.

Are you ready to claim this part of the UU one last time before leaving this chapter? This time say it with a gentle intensity that overwhelms any lower opinions trying to corrupt your thinking. Place nothing above the spirit of this truth.

Ready?

Go!

I am marvelously made.
This is what I am.
I am marvelously made.

There could be no more practical purpose to your life than to be "true to this truth." The state of mind in which you reside always gives you the kind of world in which you reside. What kind of world will you be living in when you fashion it from your marvelously made nature?

The more receptive you are to this second part of the UU, the more receptive you'll be to part one and part three; they all link together perfectly. That's because they are all one energy.

It takes a lit candle to light another candle.
Each part of the UU is waiting to be lit by you.
Perhaps this will be the first candle you light.

Now that you better understand this part of the UU, I ask you: was there anything about yourself of which you were unaware, and now you are most definitely aware? Awesome!

Let's move on to the final part of the UU…

chapter 7

Reveal, Feel, and Share

COMING TO KNOW *WHY* YOU ARE HERE

Everything in the world is organically set up "to serve." The mountain spring serves the river, which serves the ocean, which serves the algae, which serves fish, which serve mammals, and on it goes. Serving is the connecting thread that runs through everything on this planet.

Receiving and serving are also inseparable. The vast ocean receives its water from the rivers and gives it back to the sky through evaporation, which then returns it to the rivers as rain. The circle of serving and receiving never ends. The stars, the planets, the solar systems, the galaxies, the entire universe depends on it.

Now let's look at you. What better way could there be for you to serve and receive than to share your good and beautiful nature with the world? You cannot help but beautify your world when you share your abundant richness. There's an immediate bonus that comes with that. You bless yourself with your beneficence as you bless the world with it. Straight away, you receive an experience of great value—you instantly feel good about yourself. It's all part of the grand cosmic symphony.

The best of life always comes when we realize that our greatest experiences of satisfaction are when we're serving and sharing, not when we're just receiving.

Another reason that there's nothing more satisfying than sharing one's beautiful nature in increasing measures, is because there's nothing more gratifying than experiencing one's beautiful nature in increasing measures.

> Sharing and receiving is the formula for perfect living.
> Sharing is what keeps you growing.
> Receiving is what has you glowing!

The mood has been set; let's decree the third part of the Ultimate Understanding the way an enthusiastic child would decree it. Say it out of deep appreciation for the truth it offers you. As you speak the words, feel the artistry of what you are decreeing.

> *I am here to reveal, feel, and share all that is*
> *good and beautiful about me.*
> *This is why I am here.*
> *I am here to reveal, feel, and share all that is*
> *good and beautiful about me.*

Hear ye, hear ye! Your life is meant to be a festive, creative act. What better way to rejoice in life than to be in joyful service to life by going on hot streaks of spontaneous expression? You are here to celebrate your life, and you cannot do that until you move beyond the shallows, into the depths of yourself. That's when your inherent power of creative expression naturally comes to full blossom.

Expressing and experiencing *why* you are here may be like listening to unusual music at first, and can feel like trying to remember the dance steps to your favorite song from 1,000 lifetimes ago. While it may seem unfamiliar, the more you listen and dance, the more you find yourself swirling and swaying to what you hear. If you were to remain open and receptive to such moments, the next thing you know, you'll be sashaying through life in astonishing style.

Watch children joyously share themselves in the world. Their inventive nature artfully brings out all that is good and beautiful about them, as they generously contribute all of themself to everyone in the room. It is how they are thrown to be, like a crocus in spring, popping through the last groundcover of winter snow, ready to show and ready to grow. It is how *you* are thrown to be.

In your childhood moments of glee, you were an untainted expression of your *lost chord*—singing and dancing, swirling and swaying on the living room rug for everyone to see. With every sincere effort you expend to think this way, you bring yourself a little closer to being this way once again.

WHAT'S YOUR SPECIALTY?

During my teen years, I tried desperately to fit in: same haircut, same dress code, same language patterns, same physiology—there was nothing in my personality that rang of exclusivity. One day my uncle Fred sat me down and said, "*Do your thing*, Bobby. *Your thing!* Don't let your friends tell you who you should be when you're strutting your stuff."

Now I ask you, "Are you doing *your thing*?" Doing your thing is what lifts you on strong wings, above any decisions you've made to just "look good and fit in." You are a unique individual with your own specialties that are ever waiting to strengthen in your personality so they might press themselves outwardly.

The only way to sow these seeds of truth, is by releasing yourself into life completely. When you do this, you show up on the planet like a wondrous star, a unique energy from another galaxy, offering your one-of-a-kind flare.

As mentioned earlier, being yourself is always risky business in a world that insists you be who *they* want you to be. Take the risk! It's worth it! You cannot help but get a kick out of yourself when you let your hair down and reveal yourself. Never assume you have nothing to give. To do so does you a grave injustice. Have you noticed?

> It is ebulliently encouraging to probe deeper within yourself.
> Never spare yourself when you feel that calling.
> Even a small eagerness to reveal a talent that is fresh and new
> Can become the beginning of a great discovery.
> Grant permission to that eagerness
> And you'll set your mind ablaze with curiosity,
> Which rouses you to dip ever deeper
> Into your bottomless well of immeasurable capacities.

When you probe deeper into yourself, and dance in harmony with the world in which you live, life beats her tambourine gently, opening to you completely, and a supreme feeling of vibrant buoyancy comes over you.

Is your mind resisting what you're reading right now? If so, that's because you're reading through the lens of yesterday's *miss-understandings*, which will insist that none of this is true. Don't buy it, for if you do, your hidden beauty will remain hidden.

If you're to embrace life and feel fully alive, it's vital that you look at yourself with fresh, new eyes, so you may come to fresh, new conclusions about *why* you are here and what you intend to do. Of one thing you can be certain: when your beautiful nature becomes your reality, it sheds light on any areas of darkness that your past *miss-understandings* have been casting over your future.

Let's claim this part of the UU again. Be sure to allow your passion to be the heart of your expression. Your earnestness will beget your eagerness to express what you are claiming.

Ready?

I am here to reveal, feel, and share all that is
good and beautiful about me.
This is why I am here.
I am here to reveal, feel, and share all that is
good and beautiful about me.

Did you immobilize your focus on the words you just spoke? Did you monopolize your attention with the statement, "This is *why* I am here?" Let not one word of this communication be distant from you, for what you hold dearly, you cannot help but take personally—and you want to take this personally.

Here are two examples of individuals who love their lives because they love expressing what they love about themselves. Notice what they have in common:

JOANNE

Joanne is a wonderfully receptive listener. She has a knack for responding earnestly to what people share with her, so they feel good. It's one of her special gifts. Is Joanne popular? You bet! No matter where she goes, folks flock to her.

Ask Joanne her secret and she will tell you, "I always find something beautiful in what others share with me, so I can reflect it back in a way that they feel heard. I love doing that."

TOM

Tom is a middle-school counselor who is patient and kind, which is very apparent when he's working with his students. Their parents call him "The Kid Whisperer" because they see the wonderful influence he is when helping their kids work through their problems.

Ask Tom what he loves most about his job and he will tell you, "If I can help one kid experience himself without that *put-down voice* chattering in his head, I've had a fabulous day. That's what I love."

What Joanne and Tom have in common is they have discovered beautiful qualities within themselves, and they love sharing those qualities with their world. They both champion the secret to *bountiful living*, which is *bountiful giving*.

This part of the UU helps you see yourself as the flowing sea of unimaginable possibilities you're meant to be; possibilities that are always prancing within you and need but a little prodding to drift out softly or leap out joyfully.

Are you willing to be aware of yourself and share yourself as Joanne and Tom do? If you are, I guarantee you'll experience a sublime sunset at the end of each day, as do they.

IT WORKS!

Some call it "karma." Others call it "cause and effect." And still others call it the "Law of Attraction." No matter what you call it, it works with impeccable precision when you share your rich bounty with life, and consequently experience life's rich bounty in return.

When you express yourself in the world from the warmth of your generous spirit, living a life of joyful expression becomes your "karma." And when you make it a habit to live this way, you raise yourself up not once, but continually, so you can bask in the truth of *why* you are here.

And yet another bonus comes when your heart's a-throb with giving more of yourself to your world—you find that even your stumbling efforts offer you great growth and satisfaction.

NO AGE RESTRICTIONS

Do you think you're too late for the party because you are 50 or 60 or 80? Think again! Your whole world can be a place to dance or a place to stumble. When you step onto the dance floor of life with an attitude of sharing your dance with others, no matter what your age may be, your experiences of tripping the light fantastic increases exponentially. Life is generously wise and always ready to follow your lead. Worry not about stumbling.

Grandma Moses, in her late 70s, opened her mind to sublime new visions. She considered her outer world a perfect playground where she could share her inner beauty. It was then that she stirred her passion for pastoral painting. She continued to express her artistry well into her 90s. Her paintings continue to grow in popularity today. They sell for over a million dollars.

Are you ready to claim the last part of the UU one more time before leaving this chapter? Decree your communiqué with a sense of certainty that breaks through any wall of separation that may still be hindering you.

Don't slouch with your inflections.

Speak the words in a dignified manner.

Okay, here we go.

> *I am here to reveal, feel, and share all that is*
> *good and beautiful about me.*
> *This is why I am here.*
> *I am here to reveal, feel, and share all that is*
> *good and beautiful about me.*

Learn to be a committed listener when speaking to yourself this way. Your enthusiasm will never betray you. Be kind to yourself. Trust your enthusiasm. Let these words be fundamental to your self-talk when you get up in the morning. You'll be wonderfully surprised with how they will enhance your self-respect, strengthen your self-esteem, and amplify your unique presence on the planet.

Now that you know *why* you are here, I ask you: is there anything about yourself that you *already* knew, but it wasn't quite clear that you knew it, and now you clearly know it? Is there anything else about yourself that you were not aware of, that has suddenly come to light?

Allow yourself to be with the above questions for a moment before we advance once again. Let's look at another indispensable slice of this pie...

chapter 8

The Critical Addendum

DON'T MISS IT!

Indeed, you are a rich and majestic child of infinite intelligence. However, that truth is only as reliable as *you* are. Things turned out in your life the way they turned out because you've turned out in life the way *you've* turned out. If you're to take full advantage of the Ultimate Understanding, so that your life turns out the way you want it to, it's vitally important I call your attention to this Critical Addendum to the UU.

The creative intention behind the UU is lost if you just pay it lip service, and don't take responsibility for the words you are speaking. The Critical Addendum spotlights that point.

CRITICAL ADDENDUM
TO THE
ULTIMATE UNDERSTANDING

I am a rich and majestic child of infinite intelligence.
I am destined to win at whatever I set my mind to
and
I am worthy of all that is good and beautiful.

The second line of the Addendum emphasizes the importance of holding yourself accountable for the thoughts you keep and the words you speak. You awaken your dozing energy when you consciously set your mind to goals that are important to you, and you act with creative intention to achieve what you conceive. In that state of mind, opportunities increase greatly when it's time to convert your visions into reality.

You are always destined to win at what you set your mind to. So now the question becomes, "Have you set your mind to winning in life, or to whining about life?" Setting your mind to winning has you experiencing fulfilling relationships and making a positive difference in the world. Setting your mind to whining has you playing the role of helpless victim.

The problem with setting your mind to whining is that you do win, but you "win at losing" at the game of life. That's because that is all that whining can offer you.

An awakened person once commented, "I've heard of robbers on the roadside of life, but now I know the truth: *the only robber is me*." When you set your mind to whining, that's when you are the robber, *robbing* yourself of life's rich abundance.

Taking responsibility for being the only real robber in your life, is a superb start to a new beginning. Think about that for a moment. Did any dismissive thought-voice try to make hay of that idea? That voice is another form of a robber on the roadside of your life.

Let's look at the Critical Addendum again, but this time let's pay attention to the last line.

I am a rich and majestic child of infinite intelligence.
I am destined to win at whatever I set my mind to
and
I am worthy of all that is good and beautiful.

The last line alerts you to the importance of knowing that you are deserving of a rich and satisfying life. Any opinions you're holding that inhibit you from thinking that way will most assuredly close you off to experiencing your life that way. That's another form of a robber on the roadside of your life

Have you heard the statement: "You must leave home to come home"? Well, if you are to return home to the UU, you must leave your uncomfortable psychological home you call your "comfort zone" with those familiar, but routine, litany of complaints you constantly kick around. That is the home that has you feeling lost and homeless. It's the home in which the *intruder* dwells.

The more fearlessly committed you are to creating your life anew, the more obvious the last two lines of the Critical Addendum become to you. That kind of commitment invites moments of personal expansion that will continually prove the UU to be valid and true.

Let's speak the Critical Addendum aloud together.

Breathe in and out slowly.

Relax.

Take a moment to ruminate on the whole message as we speak it.

Are you ready?

> *I am a rich and majestic child of infinite intelligence.*
> *I am destined to win at whatever I set my mind to*
> *and*
> *I am worthy of all that is good and beautiful.*

Meditate on what you've just spoken for a moment. Allow its truths to sink in. Is it becoming clear that your life has only gone awry because you've allowed your mind to go awry? That clarity creates space for corrections that can quickly set your thoughts, words, and actions in the right direction.

> They are told they are worthy and powerful.
> This confuses them.
> Choked are their voices as they try to accept their worthiness.
> Many lie asleep in the darkness,
> While others begin to awaken.

You lie asleep in the darkness when you doubt you are worthy of winning, and *that doubt* becomes your expression of faith. You've placed your faith on the wrong side of the line, and all your efforts to win will *never* help you win when you place your faith in doubt. There's only *one robber* on the road you travel, and that's the doubting you.

> As you think, you travel;
> as you love you attract.
> You are today where your thoughts have brought you;
> you will be tomorrow where your thoughts take you.
>
> —James Allen[13]

73

You become aware of your power of creation when you are awake to where your thoughts have taken you. You access that power the moment you hold yourself accountable for living the life you dream of experiencing. And that begins when you know that you are today where your thoughts have brought you, and you are responsible for where your thoughts take you tomorrow.

LET'S CHECK IN

You are, right now, on the edge of the high diving board with nothing stopping you from leaping into your immense pool of monumental potential. Yes, indeed, you are a rich and majestic child of infinite intelligence. However, that alone does not guarantee you a rich and productive life. Your potential is useless if you're not willing to take the leap.

> You are the artist.
> Your life is your work of art.
> Your art is never the same as it was yesterday.
> You are never the same artist from day to day.

Are you coachable? Does what you're reading tantalize you? So many possibilities! The more you trust yourself, the more luminous your brain becomes with dazzling visions of winning.

What might you say to yourself right now that would empower you to remove the robber from the roadside of your life? Let not a single beautiful thought about yourself wither on the vine.

Change is an indisputable constant in life, and you can have a big say in what those changes will entail. As a marvelously made being, you are fully equipped to take one leap after another toward the life you dream of experiencing. A willingness to learn more about how to do this will develop your capacity to do this.

Okay, let's combine the Ultimate Understanding with the Critical Addendum.

Take a moment to bask in fruitful silence before speaking them together. Speaking them together and feeling the realness of what they offer, is to experience what you already are and have always been. A strong desire to embrace the messages they offer is all that's needed to begin.

Breathe in.
Count to four.
Breathe out.
Ready?

THE ULTIMATE UNDERSTANDING
AND
THE CRITICAL ADDENDUM

I am a rich and majestic child of infinite intelligence.
I am marvelously made.
I am here to reveal, feel, and share
all that is good and beautiful about me.
Furthermore,
I am destined to win at whatever I set my mind to
and
I am worthy of all that is good and beautiful.

When you combine the Ultimate Understanding with the Critical Addendum, you are combining the *spiritual* with the *practical*. When speaking the UU, you are speaking in spiritual terms about yourself and your destiny, and those words have a positive and practical impact on your actions. And when you speak the Critical Addendum, you hold yourself accountable for the UU, hence, your action is concise and your outcomes are precise.

It takes a lot less effort to achieve what you're conceiving when you hold in esteem these spiritual truths you are now uncovering. It is not enough to sense the validity of these messages, you must be willing to show evidence of them in your life. In this mindset, your ardor intensifies as you begin experiencing the UU and Critical Addendum in greater depth, which gives you supreme insights into your marvelously made nature.

Are you ready to even explore more of yourself?

Then you are ready for a makeover…

chapter 9

A Dynamic *To-Be* List

FAITH AND FATE

This is the chapter where you begin to put this together. Let's look at the idea of "faith" for a moment. Your faith and your fate are undeniably intertwined. Your faith in yourself has everything to do with your fate in the world. Having right-faith in yourself guarantees a fate filled with expressions of all that is good and beautiful about you.

On the other hand, *blind faith* is a blind guide. It's based on faulty reasoning stemming from childhood *miss-understandings* that leave you with "wishing and hoping," but that kind of hoping ultimately leads to the feeling of hopelessness, which guarantees more problems.

Great moment for a quick analogy: it has been proven that the heat of a forest fire serves as a catalyst for the seeds lying dormant in the cones of a lodgepole pine tree. When the cones burst open from the heat, the seeds are released, and some grow into 150-foot-tall trees. Also, that same heat of the forest fire removes years of debris from the ground; debris that would prevent the seeds from sprouting and growing.

You may be wondering what the heat of a forest fire and the cone of a lodgepole pine have to do with this conversation. Just this: the heat of your passion to know all about yourself serves as a catalyst, which begins the process of removing the debris that comes from those *miss-understandings* that sit in your field of consciousness. And that same heat calls forth your faith in yourself, which energizes those thought-seeds—those many rousing

"I AMs" you so yearn to experience—lying dormant in your subconscious, so they may sprout and grow strong in your life.

An important part of the package of being a human being is your ability to self-reflect so you may self-select, which is to look at yourself and think about yourself differently. With a newly selected "I AM," you can present a new facet of yourself to the world and reinforce it with action that supports it.

Your unique self-hood unfolds from your many self-proclaimed, "I AMs." There are millions of "ways of being" that are available. To think of yourself in a new way, prepares you for opportunities to be that way, and you'll find possibilities everywhere you look.

You are the way you are right now because of your current "I AMs," and you will be who you come to be tomorrow when you claim new "I AMs."

Claiming new "I AMs" opens you to be better understood by yourself. Nothing is more exciting than this business of learning more about your remarkable capacities, and growing from that.

Long ago, it was written that we should give beauty for ashes and praise for the spirit of heaviness.[14] When you embrace the Ultimate Understanding, you are elevating your level of thinking where you give praise for the spirit of heaviness. This potentiates your ability to have right-faith in yourself, so you can give beauty for the ashes you've experienced in your past—those *miss-understandings* that have misled you. That alone arouses many illustrious thought-seeds that are lying dormant in your consciousness.

A perfect way to initiate this process of giving praise for the spirit of heaviness is to establish a deliberate and well thought out *To-Be* list.

YOUR LIST

A well thought-out *To-Be* list is a list of consciously claimed "I AMs" that call forth new qualities, talents, and strengths within you. This gives you something of extraordinary value—unlimited opportunities to experience what it means to be a marvelously made being. Never underestimate the importance of such a list.

Your *To-Be* list is the consummate first step toward revealing your good and beautiful nature, both to yourself and to the world. And more options are made available when you add more "I AMs" to your list.

Perhaps you weren't aware of it, but you already have such a list!

Your current *To-Be* list consists of the multiple "I AMs" that you've already claimed, be those claims consciously or unconsciously made. And that list interprets you. It supports your everyday dispositions and demeanors, and all that makes up your unique individualism. That list also determines what's possible and what's impossible for you to do in the world today. Furthermore, it opens you to future opportunities, or closes them down.

Whether you put your *To-Be* list together consciously or unconsciously is important to understand, but what really matters is to know that you can alter your list and add to it. Every time you do this, you give new meaning to yourself, and that alters how you occur for yourself, which immediately alters how your world occurs for you, which alters your action in the world. Whew!

Knowing you can add to your *To-Be* list offers you the chance to notice the qualities you envy in others, so you may polish those qualities up in yourself, and put them on display in your life.

Can you see the remarkable value of consciously choosing your "I AMs," rather than making those choices randomly? If you want your future to be filled with experiences that are fresh and new, you must take the time to design your "I AMs" so they take you beyond the 'usual you.'

Consider your *To-Be* list as your *possibilities list*. The more "new ways of being" you add to your list, the more prospects you find available for a life of joyous growth and expansion. One thing is certain: if you don't make any changes to your *To-Be* list, your future will look like your past. That's because it will be a product of your past "I AMs."

ONTOLOGICAL QUERY

Ontology is a branch of philosophy that deals with the *nature of being*. In moments of solo self-reflection, you are aware of yourself as a *self* with specific "ways of being." Your "I AMs" characterize those "ways" that you consider yourself to be.

When an "I AM" makes sense to you, that means it fits in with the other "I AMs" already on your *To-Be* list. When it doesn't make sense, it means it doesn't fit in yet. However, that doesn't necessarily mean you have to toss it out. You can test it out if you want to, and perhaps you'll find it to be a better fit for who you *now* want to be.

You can also remove "I AMs" from your *To-Be* list. It's wise to do that when you find one that no longer serves you. That's what I refer to as dying of the old to create space for something new to sprout through.

Whenever you see yourself being "this way" or "that way," and you shift your attention to quite another "I AM"—in that moment you begin expressing yourself differently. For example: you are angry with someone ("I am angry"), and then that person explains what happened and you earnestly forgive them ("I am forgiving"). How did that happen? You shifted your attention from one "I AM" to another. It's that simple.

You are an opening for uncountable capabilities when it comes to "I AMs." Being a human being endows you with *unlimited ways of being*.

Wow! To be or not to be!

Now imagine organizing your *To-Be* list with "I AMs" that fully support you. There would be no surprises when it came time to release more of your talents and strengths into your life. Can you see the importance of intentionally composing your *To-Be* list?

CONCLUSIVE SUCCESS FORMULA

If you plan to be successful in life, "Being to Doing to Having" is the only way to go. If you're going to confidently conceive yourself achieving what you are perceiving, it all starts with who you are *Being*. Hence, any formula for success worth its salt has a direct progression from *Being,* and then to *Doing,* and then to *Having*.

We learn early in life how to compose a *To-Do* list in order to get things done. However, few folks know that they've jumped in the middle of the process, and left the essential first part out.

You need a supportive *To-Be* list to guarantee your *To-Do* list gets done. Only when you are *Being* who you need to be, in order to achieve what you're conceiving, can you do what needs *Doing* so you can enjoy *Having* what you're perceiving. That is the only "for-sure" route to take.

Yup, it's that simple. When you put *"Doing"* before *"Being"* when endeavoring to succeed, you end up with a lot of striving and trying, which lacks the necessary passion and direction. When Yoda said to Luke Skywalker, "Do. Or do not. There is no try,"[15] he was alluding to the fact that effective *Doing* is not about trying, it's about who you are *Being*.

Your *To-Be* list should consist of "I AMs" that inspire confidence in you so you act with conviction when it's time to do what needs doing to complete your *To-Do* list, or your bucket list. When you get your *Beingness* right, you no longer nervously strive, you simply do what needs *Doing* with invincible might.

Furthermore, a truly effective *To-Be* list contains "I AMs" that not only enhance your chances of accomplishing your *To-Do* list, but also lessen the time required to accomplish it. Establish who you need *To Be*, and the *doing* comes naturally, which then takes less time to complete.

Can you recall a time when you conceived yourself achieving what you perceived, and then proceeded to do what was needed? Do you remember how there was no pushy trying-effort involved? Well, here's what happened: in the process of conceiving yourself achieving what you were perceiving—you passed through a twilight of mild fervor, then into a dawning of exuberant confidence, and finally into buoyant enthusiasm. That is the hope of all mankind. Can you recall such a time? Perhaps you did it unconsciously, but you had to have claimed an "I AM" that made all that possible for you.

Your life has worked out the way it has worked out because of your current *To-Be* list. If your life has not worked out as you hoped it would, that's because your *To-Be* list was missing the "I AMs" necessary for you to do what needed to be done.

If you're going to take your future seriously, you cannot afford to assume things will "just happen" in your favor. Your *To-Be* list should always support you with your goals and aspirations. You need not live in a dry desert, in a parched state of insufficiency. No longer be stingy with yourself when it's time to claim "I AMs" that express all that is beautiful about you.

CONSCIOUSLY COMPOSE

There are unfathomable, unseen, brilliant planets in the heavens, just as there are unfathomable, unseen, brilliant qualities in your heavenly state of being. Weigh in carefully with what you are reading. When you take even a little effort to actively monitor and adjust your *To-Be* list, you reveal more of your brilliant qualities. A well organized *To-Be* list gives you an expanded awareness of your many dimensions of being.

The sum total of "I AMs" you've placed on your *To-Be* list is the sum total of character traits that you currently display through your personality. Constructing an empowering *To-Be* list, and embracing that list with intentionality, cultivates a personality that serves you unconditionally.

The productive "I AMs" you've placed on your *To-Be* list make up your pleasing personality. The unproductive "I AMs" make up that other personality, imposed on you by the *intruder*.

You are the ultimate authority when it comes to what's on your *To-Be* list. You have complete jurisdiction over your "I AMs." Every time you exercise your authority by responsibly altering your *To-Be* list, you create space for more innovation and ingenuity.

Let's look at how to consciously compose your *To-Be* list.

Here are three questions to kindle your flame of curiosity when it comes to determining who you will be:

1. What current "I AMs," on my *To-Be* list support *me*?

2. What "I AMs" should I add that will have me explore more of life?

3. What "I AMs" should I add that would help me solve the problems I'm stuck with?

4. What "I AMs" should I delete from the list that are hampering me?

If you make it a habit of asking yourself questions like these, they will alert you to changes you may want to consider when it comes to your list.

Here are a few examples of supportive "I AMs" (from A to I):

I am affable.	I am delightful.	I am generous.
I am bold.	I am elegant.	I am helpful.
I am capable.	I am fun.	I am interesting.

If you were to jot down your current *To-Be* list alphabetically, what qualities of character are *already* glowing and demonstrating themselves in your personality? Just let it flow. What shows up for you?

I am _____	I am _____	I am _____
I am _____	I am _____	I am _____
I am _____	I am _____	I am _____

This is important work you're doing. You are making distinctions about yourself that offer new ways of seeing yourself that create clearings for new ways of being yourself. A gradual expansion of a series of new distinctions gives you a whole new world in which to live.

With your above *To-Be* list in mind, what's missing? What distinctions would you like to introduce yourself to today? Remember, you are not creating new virtues from scratch, but redeeming them from your unused batch. Think of this as a fascinating "virtues scavenger hunt."

Knowing your "I AMS" are calling you to be, what do you want them to call you to be? Always write them in the first person, present tense, and write them like they are ways of being that you would truly enjoy expressing. They are not hollow platitudes, they are your future unfolding.

I am _____ I am _____ I am _____
I am _____ I am _____ I am _____
I am _____ I am _____ I am _____

Can you think of a time when you made a distinction about yourself in order to accomplish something new? You've done it a thousand times, otherwise you would not have evolved from a toddler to a fully functioning adult.

Just to remind you—with a new *To-Be* list you do not actually reinvent yourself or create your *self* anew. What you're doing is resurrecting unexpressed aspects of yourself that have always been available, aspects that augment your ability to succeed with your aims and aspirations.

YOUR CONCEPTIONS

All of your current "I AMs" are your conceptions of yourself, brought to light with external demonstrations. The external demonstrations call upon the quality contained in the "I AMs."

The only thing prohibiting you from energizing a new quality of character in your personality—be it patience, persistence, spontaneity, playfulness—is a *miss-understanding* that insists you don't possess it.

So, hear this now:

There is no coal of character
so dead that it won't glow and flame
if but slightly turned.

—Neville Goddard[16]

You, and only you, have the power to slightly turn a new coal of character so it may glow and flame within you. When you do that effectively, that coal of character glows inwardly and radiates outwardly for the whole world to see.

How do you slightly turn one of those coals of character? After having deliberately added that "I AM" to your *To-Be* list, go out in the world and behave in ways that support it. When you energize an "I AM," that quality becomes part of your psychology. That's when your confidence skyrockets, and your demonstration of that "I AM" is right on point. That's also when any *miss-understanding* that opposes that "I AM" loses its clout, no matter how loud that thought-voice may shout.

Think of your new "ways of being" like muscles. If you want them to grow strong, you have to exercise them. The more attention you give to a new "way of being," the stronger it develops, just like a well-exercised muscle. (This is covered in detail, later in the book.)

Let's look at your new *To-Be* list again. You did the exercise, didn't you? Are there any other qualities you want to give an opportunity to demonstrate through you?

SASS

"I faced it all and I stood tall and did it my way." Those lyrics, from the song *My Way*, made famous by Frank Sinatra, remind me of the importance of consciously creating a *To-Be* list that supports you. The only way to do your life "your way" is to stand tall and face it all with a *To-Be* list that empowers you to handle whatever life may toss your way.

Sometimes you've got to add a little sass, when embracing a new "way of being." That's especially true when your old ways of reasoning try to discourage you. Sass helps you to step beyond your cramped mind. Frank Sinatra was a great example of sass.

Your inspiring "I AMs" encourage you always; they never let you down. When in that state of mind, if you find yourself stumbling, you recover gracefully, like a butterfly learning to use its wings.

All of humanity's marvelous states of being are available to you, yet not one "I AM" will ever impose itself on you. You must decide! By the way, the more conscious you become of the qualities of character you're adding to your *To-Be* list, the more obvious the reality of the Critical Addendum becomes to you.

Imagine being a gentle King Kong, sharing kindness and compassion in the world. Imagine turning those coals of character until they flame within you. Life is always conspiring to help you feel like that. Of course, life can only help you when you conspire to help yourself.

> Life's richness is illimitable.
> You are an illimitable expression of life.
> Your inner world gives you your passion to play.
> Your outer world becomes your playground.
> Your grasp of this is never too ample.

Life offers you a thousand opportunities daily to express yourself in a thousand shades of glowing colors. Life also offers you a thousand opportunities daily to express yourself in a thousand shades of gray. Your radiance glows when your "I AMs" express your beauty. You choose gray when you are ignorant of any other way.

ROB

I remember an instance where I added a new "I AM" to my *To-Be* list. I was seven, just learning to play checkers. After losing many games I finally won one while playing my sister, Buffy. "Gosh, Bobby," my father said, "you are one persistent son-of-a-gun. You just don't quit until you win." The moment Dad said this, a new coal of character began flaming within me.

After that, I played checkers with anyone who was willing, and I would play 100 games, if that's what it took to win. My father introduced me to the coal of character—*persistence*—and I bought into it completely. The mantra "I am persistent" continues to be part of my identity.

I remember another time, being in a situation where I needed to add "unruffled patience" to my *To-Be* list. I was negotiating with a business partner, and we had both grown impatient and hot-headed. The conflict in question was about holding or selling a piece of property we'd purchased several years prior.

The dispute escalated to a point where we weren't speaking. Fortunately, I could see the insanity of the situation, and it became clear to me that if we were going to resolve the matter, I had to transcend my personal limitation of being so quick to anger.

To make, "I am unruffled patience" stick, I had to be sharp and alert to moments when I reverted to my usual angry reactions. That meant I had to consciously intervene on angry thought-themes that were driving me.

The big question for me became, "Am I willing to be an expression of unruffled patience so we both win, or do I prefer to be right, no matter what the price?" How powerful we can be when we set our minds to what's truly important. I chose to be an expression of unruffled patience. We settled amicably!

Since then, there have been many more times when this "I AM" has been there for me!

If you want to predict who you will be tomorrow, simply look at what's going on with your *To-Be* list today. If who you are *being* does not support what you'd like to be *doing*, you know what you have to do: you need a makeover. That means your *To-Be* list needs a do-over, aye?

STRADIVARIUS

Imagine a magnificent Stradivarius violin, strung out of tune. That violin is a remarkable masterpiece lost in contradiction, and it wouldn't matter how skilled a violinist might be, she wouldn't be able to reveal the violin's incredible potential until she tuned it.

Well guess what? You are a remarkable masterpiece, an exquisite Stradivarius, so to speak. Are you strung out of tune? It's a shame to lose yourself in contradiction. Your job is to clarify the music you want to play, and tune yourself up with a *To-Be* list that has you playing in the right key. Move toward your lost chord as if it is in reach. It is in reach!

The more open you are to knowing more of what you do not yet consciously know about yourself, the easier it will be to express yourself authentically, with your myriad remarkable hidden talents.

Grab that pen once again. Let's approach your *To-Be* list a little differently. What is a coal of character that you admire in one of your heroes? If you were to personalize it, what "I AM" would describe it? I am _____ _____.

Alert! What thou *see-eth* in others, thou *be-eth* within. You would not admire that coal of character in your hero if it were not waiting to glow and flame within you. The reason you're noticing that quality is because it's available within you and beckoning to you. Furthermore, it's only because of a *miss-understanding* that you're still holding on to, that you're not expressing and experiencing that quality already.

Now, what about adding that coal of character to your *To-Be* list? Do you think it's mere coincidence you chose that particular hero to think about?

You are making great progress. The pace is perfect. Can you feel a superior mood coming over you? When your mood feels superior, it's easy to shine your attention on coals of character that you want shining bright until they're in plain sight in your life. With that right mood in mind, what else do you perceive yourself to be in your finest hours? Add that to your *To-Be* list!

THE WIND IS BLOWING

You are a sailor on the great ocean of life. The wind is blowing. Your mainsail is up. Your hands are on the rudder. The rudder awaits your direction. To sail beyond old, familiar waters you must stop clinging to old moorings. How are you to turn your rudder in a new direction, and sail out onto the vast blue sea—where there are sunny skies and colorful rainbows—if you insist on being the same ol' sailor you've always been?

Dare to sail into what's possible today, and most definitely there will be even more possibilities tomorrow. Perhaps you don't know it yet, but these guided imaginings I am offering are sinking in softly.

> Oh wondrous, so wondrous is this child of the infinite.
> Oh glorious, so glorious is this marvelously made being.
> Can you hear that calling?
> The heavens are speaking about you.
> Throw your whole self into a love affair with revealing yourself.
> Listen to the throbbing of your heart.
> Give from your richness generously.

Never will you experience your wondrous nature by being miserly. You are a golden tone, meant to chime magnificently in this grand, cosmic orchestra. Nothing is more rewarding than to consciously participate.

Appreciating yourself as an illimitable expression of the infinite enables you to crack any remaining shell of insufficiency in which you have encased yourself. And as the shell cracks wide, you will experience what the newborn falcon feels when breaking free of its egg—an incredible compulsion to unfold its wings and experience meritorious feats of flight.

THERE YOU HAVE IT

Perhaps you're thinking, "What could possibly stop me from closing the book right now? It seems I have all I need to experience an incredible life."

- I've been introduced to the Ultimate Understanding.
- I've learned the significance of the Critical Addendum.
- I now know the importance of creating a *To-Be* list.

Might I say to you, "Hold on! Despite all you've read, I must warn you—there's resistance up ahead!" Being exposed to the truth does not immediately rid your mind of booby traps. For years, your subconscious has been peppered with land mines, triggered to blow whenever you entertain something new about yourself.

If the truth is to shine brightly in your field of consciousness you must confront those spellbinding thought-patterns that throw you into darkness. Here ye, the good news—those negative charges can be defused.

Are you ready to look at what has gone wrong, with an eye for making it right? You cannot make it right until you look right at it to see what needs correcting. If your answer is "Yes," then get ready! It's time to reveal that ruthless *intruder* who constantly robs you of your life.

Let's move on to Part Two…

PART TWO

seeing it like it is without
making it worse

chapter 10

The *Intruder*

DUELING IDENTITIES

This is a critical juncture in our expedition. In the practice of Zen, they speak of traveling the low road to get to the high road. It seems traveling the low road is filled with potholes. It's also the road that *never* takes us where we want to go.

> Why would anyone travel the low road?
> Why would *you* travel that road?
> Because there's not one of you traveling—but two!

Yes, you have two selves behind the wheel of your vehicle, two selves with which you identify. And these two selves give you hugely different experiences of yourself and your world.

There is the authentic you, which I refer to as the Maestro.

This is the "self" that conducts your daily affairs and orchestrates your life so it unfolds like an exquisite symphony. The Maestro places you on the high road. You'll become fully acquainted with this ingenious composer in Chapter 18.

There is also the *other self*, which I refer to as the *intruder*.

The *intruder* is an imposter, always ready to use your life for high drama. This is the unwanted mental houseguest that hijacks your potential and uses it unproductively. The *intruder* places you on the low road.

You innocently gave birth to, and breathed life into, this *other self* during childhood moments of distress and discomfort, as you began identifying with flawed assumptions that arose from your *miss-understandings*. The sole substance of the *intruder* is the collection of flawed assumptions that gained prominence in your belief system and eminence in your personality.

Unfortunately, the more you responded to life from these flawed assumptions, the more life you breathed into your assumptive identity—the *intruder*. And what's worse—the more life you breathed into this identity, the deeper you buried the Maestro in your consciousness.

It's a remarkably awakening experience to subject this *other self* to analysis. For it's a startling moment to realize that you've submitted your *will* to such a conditioned state of being. Are you ready to meet this *other self* that was born a couple years after you were born?

Let's look at what we're dealing with here:

- The *intruder* is a flawed hallucination, an abstraction that you breathed life into.
- This flawed hallucination is a *great pretender* that has convinced you and the world that it is the real you.
- This abstraction has had almost as many birthdays as you; that's how long it has been with you.

Once you recognize this imposter as nothing more than a counterfeit version of you that you put into action, you open the door that leads to many other doors that you'll love opening and walking through.

The *intruder*, the *other self*, the *imposter*, the *great pretender*, your assumptive identity—all describe the same confused human condition. This *imposter's* entire presence is rooted in your programmed mind, ruled by memories of distress and discomfort. Being defensive and reactive are two of the *intruder's* favorite postures.

> Your *intruder* is a low-level thinker.
> It's not programmed to grow vertically or climb upwardly.

Hence your unrealized potential remains unrealized,
And your hidden talents remain hidden.

When the *intruder* is running your affairs, you can be sure there's a lot of drama. So how do you rid yourself of this assumptive entity? Well, the odd thing is—there's nothing you need to do…but *be yourself*. However, after allowing the *intruder* to live these many years *as you*, just "being yourself" can be a challenge.

Strange but true! Even though life always grants you the space to be who you want to be, you cannot live in that space freely until you stop taking the *intruder* so personally. On the positive side—when you do learn to see through this conditioned state of being, the truth you find is incredibly freeing.

IT'S SNEAKY

The *intruder* is sneaky. There's no doubt about that. It does not want you looking directly at it because it cannot afford to be exposed to the light of truth. It's like a vampire that shuns the light as it sucks the lifeblood out of its victim. However, the *intruder* can only do that to you when you're not mindful of it.

The *intruder* is very tricky. It can only survive by pointing your spotlight of attention into the darkness. Hence, if you look at it directly, it will immediately be self-justifying, and do whatever it must do, to convince you that it is you. That's why this *other self* is also known as the *great pretender*, because it is so expert at convincing *you* and *everyone else* that it is you. If only you knew how many millions of times you've fallen into the trap of mistaking this *other self* as the authentic you.

So what to do?

The moment you stop anthropomorphizing this *great pretender* is the moment you stop assuming it is you. A great way to impersonalize it is to call it—*"it."* That's when it becomes obvious that *"it"* is nothing more than a deceptive illusion that has set up camp in your consciousness.

Socrates offered fabulous advice with his words, "Man, know thyself."[17] This maxim—*Gnothi Seauton*—was engraved on the temple of Apollo at Delphi, 2,500 years ago, during the Golden Age of Greece…yet here we are, still stuck with *"it."*

Since the beginning of civilization, "knowing thyself" incorrectly has caused humanity's esteem to plummet 1,000 leagues under a sea of faulty assumptions. Similarly, Shakespeare also tried to wake us up when he wrote, "To thine own self be true."[18]

Both Socrates and Shakespeare were referring to the self that displays the marvelously made you. They emphasized the importance of your original nature because they were fully aware of "*it*" and *its* many deceptive practices.

Again, I remind you that *it* will do whatever is necessary to stop you from seeing *it* for the menacing shadow *it* is. When you experience inner contradictions that cause indecision after indecision, it's time to suspect that *it* is having *its* way with you. And when *it's* having *its* way, you can be damn sure, you are *not* being true to yourself.

> The tragedy of life is not death;
> rather, it is what we let die inside of us while we live.
>
> —Norman Cousins[19]

When we're not true to ourselves we allow our remarkable aptitudes to die within us. As you can see, you cannot afford to allow the *intruder* to have *its* say, not if you intend to experience the marvelously made being that you are.

Another important fact to note is that this *other self* is the only power you ever really compete with in the world. Just knowing that opens up a little breathing room. When you become aware that you were unaware of this *imposter*, posing as you, it's obvious that there's nothing "out there" in the world that can stop you from living your dreams like the *intruder* can.

WHO SHUT THE DOOR?

During moments of childhood failure and fear you innocently shut the door on the Ultimate Understanding. Had you not shut that door, the door for the *intruder* would never have opened, which made embracing the UU such a Herculean task.

Your programmed mental machinery turns its cogs mindlessly, making you react mechanically. This state of mind displays an *obvious absence* of spontaneity and creativity.

> *Miss-understandings* beget toxic emotions.
> Toxic emotions beget faulty self-opinions.
> Faulty self-opinions beget limiting decisions.
> Limiting decisions beget unproductive behavior.
> Unproductive behavior supports your *miss-understandings*.
> That is the *intruder's* life cycle in motion.

The more you are willing to adventure into the noisy wasteland of the mechanical mind to discover who you are *not*, the sooner you will find yourself journeying homeward to the quiet meadow where your authenticity awaits. However, be warned! Your *intruder* will push back like a mighty wind, for it has its own *To-Be* list to protect.

TWO LISTS!

There is no wiggle room here, you have two selves, and each has its own *To-Be* list. Your "way of being" in the world is energized by the list you are identifying with in any given moment. That list makes itself known through your personality.

Two identities; two *To-Be* lists, two personalities. All of that is *your* distinctive trademark. If you're to live from the quality *To-Be* list you put together earlier in this book—the list that places you on the high road of life—it's pertinent you make clear a distinction between the two lists.

When you express yourself from the *To-Be* list that you put together when feeling good about yourself, what shines through your personality are those virtues that support a rich reality filled with many possibilities. That's the authentic you expressing.

When you express yourself from the *To-Be* list that you put together when feeling bad about yourself, your personality *poisons* your chances of feeling optimistic and confident. Now you've made your *poisonality* your trademark, which supports an impoverished reality. That's the *intruder* expressing.

Nothing renders your potential impotent like the *intruder*. When caught in *its To-Be* list, you not only believe in your *miss-understandings*, you defend them vigorously. However, nothing renders the *intruder* impotent like looking directly at *its To-Be* list so you can get to the bottom of this mess. Oh, the zeal you feel when you break free from the *intruder's To-Be* list and unseal the real deal!

Here are samples of a typical *intruder's To-Be* list, which gets a "rotten tomato" rating. You may also notice it has a lot of "nots" in it, which gives you a lot of knots in your stomach.

- I am a failure.
- I am powerless.
- I am unlovable.
- I am a victim of a harsh world.
- I am not smart.
- I am not coordinated.
- I am unworthy.
- I am inadequate.
- I am wrong.
- I am unlucky.
- I am not talented.
- I am not funny.

Oh what a terrible amnesiac state we place ourselves in when we identify with the *intruder's To-Be* list. That's when we forget all about the truth of our marvelously made nature. What has your *intruder's* To-Be list cost you? Fortunately, this amnesiac state can be *temporary*, hence forgetting who you truly are need not be permanent.

Resisting the truth of one's original nature is the low road to ruin. Cooperating with the truth is the high road to restoration. If you're to cooperate with the truth you must begin peeling away the layers of faulty "I AMs" and "I AM Nots" of which the *other self* consists.

The *peeling* process proves to be a *revealing* process, which is like stripping off layers of paint from the canvas of a counterfeit Rembrandt and discovering a Rembrandt masterpiece underneath. You blink and look again, exclaiming, "Oh, my God! What I considered valid and true was nothing more than a cheap, counterfeit version of the real thing, which has always been there, right below the surface!"

> The *other self* is a mere shadow of the marvelously made you.
> It is a shadow that cowers in the valley of darkness.
> It casts veils of doubt over every triumph you dare envision.
> You are not a counterfeit version of something marvelously made.
> You are the real thing!

The moment you begin *peeling*, you begin *revealing* the errors in judgment you've made about yourself. If you continue to peel until you reach the bottom layer of falsehoods on the *intruder's To-Be* list—poof!—this *other self* disappears. Now you're free to express "the Rembrandt" you've always been.

THE INTRUDER'S FAVORITE QUESTION

Perhaps you're wondering, "How did the *intruder* get so much clout, and how does *it* put together a *To-Be* list?" It's quite simple: the *intruder* thrives on one question: *"What's wrong with me?"* That one question, in its many forms, gives the *intruder* its *To-Be* list. This *other self* has been snowballing you with the above question since you were a child.

Its list consists of all those false assumptions you hold of yourself. With the answers to, *"What's wrong with me?"* the *intruder* gathers *its* many psychological kegs of dynamite—ever ready to blow your dreams to smithereens. There's *its* clout!

All of your tainted presumptions about yourself are psychological kegs of dynamite with short fuses. An example of a short fuse is the act of *overemphasizing* and *overapplying* (covered earlier). *It* loves high drama, and what better way to initiate high drama than to ask, *"What's wrong with me?"* That is the essence of all your emotional theatrics in life.

When the *intruder* is running your affairs, walking through life is like stepping through an imaginary minefield, tiptoeing guardedly around obstacles and traps that don't really exist. You walk gingerly, your every move slow and overcautious.

> The *other self* is an invalid identity
> Standing at the base of the mountain,
> Shaking and trembling under the shade of a tree,
> Casting veils of confusion over every challenge *it* sees.
>
> This entity single-handedly stops you
> From being the mountain climber you're here to be.
> *It's* the reason you walk through life so gingerly.

So there you have it: your feelings of helplessness do not come from the world pushing you around, but from the *intruder* pushing you around. *It* thrives on you feeling like a victim. *It* must keep your problems alive in order to thrive.

TWO SELVES, TWO WORLDS

Two very different *selves* give you two very different experiences of yourself, which give you two very different worlds to inhabit. The world you are inhabiting reflects the "self" you are projecting. It's not what you're responding *to* in life that has an impact on you, but rather the "self" you are responding *from*.

If you're to save yourself from an unsettling world, first you must save yourself from the unsettling *great pretender*, posing as you. If you act from your assumptive identity long enough, pretty soon that's all that shows. And after some time passes, the *intruder* is all you know.

It's your right to live your life to the fullest. It's your responsibility to express your aliveness. Your soul's fiercest hunger is to reveal the authentic you. This hunger never stops tugging, but beware—the *other self*, born from wrong but strong conclusions is ever ready to betray you by *denouncing* that you are marvelously made. When you listen to that *self*, you stand in your world, unstable!

> A double-minded man is unstable in all his ways.
> —James 1:8 (KJV)[20]

It's a wonderfully awakening moment to reveal how clever the *intruder's* acts of self-deception have been. We are going to continue to look at this double-minded state of being, but with an attitude of disbelief that we ever got caught in this condition. As your confidence in these truths increases, it's captivating to notice what's available when you get beyond the dispiriting reactions of the *intruder*.

Long ago, it was written, "He who has ears, let him hear."[21] You were born with an astounding capacity for hearing the truth. But unfortunately, as an innocent child, you were naïve and easily impressionable. You did not have the reasoning skills to discern truth from *miss-understandings*, and here you are now, still reacting from your faulty reasoning of childhood.

Are you beginning to feel a fondness for what you are hearing? Follow that fondness! Whenever you're feeling bulldozed to emotionally act out, that's a signal to listen deeper than what the *intruder's* telling you. The closer you get to the truth, the easier it is to hear the truth, the whole truth, and nothing but the truth.

If you watch birds take flight, they intuitively fly into the wind, knowing the "resisting energy" will lift them higher. As you continue on this voyage with me, you'll discover many ways to regard the resistance of the *other self* like the wind, and you'll uncover many ways to use that energy to lift yourself ever higher.

The only thing that is even remotely gratifying about the *intruder* is the uncomfortable feeling of comfort that comes with the familiarity of having had it around for so long. You are a rich and majestic child of infinite intelligence. You are the Maestro when it comes to shaping your "I AMs" so you can orchestrate your life as you dream it can be. Are you ready to say "Yes" to that?

YOUR QUALIFICATIONS ARE UNPARALLELED

You have the ability to flood your mental screen with vivid imaginings of who you want to be, and transform those imaginings into visions that *feeeel* real for you. Further, you are able to embody those visions in your personality and project them outwardly for the whole world to see. The objective results of your subjective creations are as obvious to the world as the cause hidden deeply within you.

Wow, think about that for a moment! You are able to manipulate the luminous energy of the cosmos into three-dimensional, holographic images of yourself. You then cast those images, in living color, onto the screen of your mind, which then projects them onto the screen of life for the whole world to see. What limit can there be when you put on your thinking cap and use this talent intelligently? Imagine how generous you could be with yourself.

On the other hand, you suffer dire consequences when you *misuse* your superior creative capacity to manipulate that luminous energy. If you knew back then what you know right now, would you have consciously assumed a false identity, one that denies the validity of your unparalleled qualifications?

> Knock, knock; opportunity is knocking.
> You are being handed a spiritual lamp.
> Energy-releasing clarity comes to you
> When you use this lamp consciously.

You are *the maker*, and you are *the made*,
You are *the conceiver*, and you are the *conception*.
You are *the creator*, and you *the creation*.
It's all *a miracle*, and you are *that miracle*.

As thou hast believed, so it is done unto thee.

—Matthew 8:13 (KJV)[22]

We've covered a lot of territory. Do you want to take a short break before looking deeper into the nature of the *intruder*? Are you willing to stay with this conversation all the way through, and continue to engage in it even when it frustrates you?

If you are ready to carry on—great!

Then pull your chair a little closer.

Let me tell you a story...

chapter 11

The Orphaned Eagle

THE PERIL OF MISIDENTIFICATION

Let me tell you a story about an orphaned eagle; see if you might find yourself somewhere in this story. A farmer found a fledgling eagle in his cornfield and placed her in the chicken coop with the barnyard hens. It wasn't long before this naïve eagle began identifying with the chickens as she began busying herself with nervous clucking and dirt-scratching.

The fledgling actually came to believe she was a barnyard hen, so much so that when the flock reacted to shadows, she would frantically scatter about with the best of them. Her mind was a clucking machine, and she became a dirt-scratching robot. She'd lowered her expectations drastically.

It took but a short period of intense conditioning by the community of chickens before the fledgling had suffered a state of temporary amnesia. And while in that state she was *not* able to see her self-limiting behavior as self-limiting, hence she could see no other option but to cluck like the others.

In my story, there's a twist. Here's what happened next. One day, a wise elder eagle flew over the chicken yard and witnessed this peculiar sight. He swooped down, cornered the fledgling, and spoke to her about her real nature.

He offered her this wise advice: "There are no limitations imposed on an eagle except those the eagle imposes on herself. To live with integrity, you must honor your authentic *eagleness* and accept nothing less. Give up the pretenses and the lies you hold about yourself. Stop camouflaging the truth.

You are a marvelously made being of an extraordinary nature. The cost of assuming you are less than that, is always your freedom!"

After listening intently, the fledgling awakened from her state of temporary amnesia and experienced a transformational moment. She responded to the elder eagle's rescuing message by rejecting her assumptive identity.

Only after she gave up the hoax of being a chicken was she able to stretch her wings and soar high into flight, with her heart pounding gleefully. No more nervous clucking, no more reactive pecking. How practical! How spiritual!

With that singular decision, the fledgling emancipated herself from her chicken yard prison by releasing her original nature and taking action, thereupon spreading her wings wide and accompanying the elder eagle high into the open sky.

GREAT LESSONS

Great lessons are often best absorbed when offered through parable. This tale of the orphaned eagle points to the conflict found in each of us. It exposes the duality of the human condition when caught in that state of self-division. An eagle divided against herself cannot stand proud as an eagle.

When you're feeling stuck, and are nervously reacting by clucking and scratching, the key to freedom is *not* gnashing your teeth or weeping and complaining. That kind of behavior, which belongs to the *intruder*, only adds more confusion to the situation.

The first step to transformation is realizing that you are cooped up in a hen-house mentality, and it's *you* who did that to yourself. Furthermore, if you've been stuck in that mental condition for years, it's *you* who tossed away the key. That knowledge alone is your Get Out of Jail Free card.

Do you remember what the wise eagle shared with the fledgling? Well, now I say to you, "There are no limitations imposed on you except those *you* impose on yourself." And the cost of those self-imposed limitations is your freedom!

When you have even a small but sincere desire to understand what we're looking at here, you have located the key to the jailhouse door. *Right here is* where that can happen. *Right now* is when it can happen. And only *you*—the Maestro—can make it happen.

The wise, elder eagle gave the fledgling permission to think higher opinions of herself by urging her to think the *unthinkable*. This required she stretch her mind beyond the chicken coop box-of-thoughts in which she was caught. That's when she answered her calling from deep within. I am now urging you to think what has been *unthinkable* for you.

No matter how far you've strayed from the truth, it's never too late to awaken. *Awakening is art in creation.* Delay no longer. The authentic you is radiantly cheerful, wonderfully resourceful, and remarkably purposeful. What could be a nobler act than to prove this to be true? Ask yourself, "Am I here to peck in the dirt for grubs or soar high in the sky?"

Are you prepared to unfold your wings? The mountain peaks are calling.

STILL CLINGING?

The only reason you would continue to cling to your assumptive identity is because of your strong, psychological drive for certainty. Once you feel certain about who you *assume* yourself to be, you fear that if you abandon that point of view you would be laid bare, and there'd be nothing there! What's there is shear possibility!

Your *other self* forever brings yesterday into today when you're contemplating tomorrow. This *self*, which is always stuck in the past, constructs today's reality from yesterday's wrong conclusions. It does this by constantly replaying yesterday's dramas and imposing those scenes onto what's happening today.

When caught in yesterday's dramas it's inevitable that you *re-act* today as you acted back then—stimulus-response, stimulus-response—same old mental movies replaying repeatedly, and you living mechanically, rather than freshly and originally. How is tomorrow to become a thrilling adventure when it's nothing more than a replay of yesterday?

The *other self's* reactive nature is *its only* nature. It takes delight in the fight to make you right about your past dramas of limit and lack. And it accomplishes this by systematically discarding any new ideas found outside the parameter in which it operates.

So, what do you feel like when you think from your creative nature? You feel like Zeus! No longer are you ruled by those self-limiting points of view that the *intruder* imposes on you. Zero limits! That has you standing tall, with your enormous potential waiting to unfold.

Ask any child what they want to do when they grow up, and they'll sail off into a vast ocean of possibilities. They leap from ballerina to astronaut in a single bound. That's because the *other self* has not yet chained their imaginations to the so-called safe harbor where the past exists.

> Are you applying what you are reading to yourself right now?
> Are you asking, "What's this got to do with me?"

When it comes to your personal evolution there is no greater challenge than to break free of living with dueling identities. Therein lies the prime reason for so many complications in your psychology. When you are passionate about knowing what you need to know so you might advance your life and grow…all of this makes sense.

> If you're to see the beauty
> Found on the summit of the mountain,
> First you must be willing to thoroughly investigate
> The dark valley that stops you from soaring.

You have access to a powerful one-two punch when it comes to this stuff…

R&R

R&R (*Recognizing* and *Real-I-zing*), is a powerful tag team. First you must *Recognize* the *great pretender* you've come to be, before you can *Real-I-ze* the astonishingly resourceful *"I"* that is found deep within you.

To *Real-I-ze*, in my dictionary, is to *make real* that authentic "I." But how are you to *Real-I-ze* if you don't *Recognize* the *great pretender* when it's in action?

Carl Jung, the founder of analytical psychology, summed this matter up wonderfully when he said, "Until you make the unconscious conscious, the unconscious directs your life, and you will call it fate." Might I remind you that it is not fate that's forcing you to live an unsatisfying life. It's your unconscious activity, breathing life into your assumptive identity.

When you deliberately step outside yourself to make the unconscious conscious, by becoming more aware of yourself, you begin noticing those familiar scenes of past failure that make you react to life today as you did yesterday. And when you notice that, you also notice—it's your reenacting those dramatic episodes continually that empowers your assumptive identity.

The *intruder* leaves clues. It is a deluded roamer. It desperately clings to the familiar by *re-acting* as it always acted. The more conscious you become of your involuntary *re-actions*, the more you *Recognize* what stops you from *Real-I-zing* your creative capacities.

This *great pretender* is indeed a thief, working in the dark of night to continually steal your life. While on this topic, I want to let you know that there is another obstacle to *Recognizing* and *Real-I-zing* the truth: that's the community in which you live. Your community will insist you continue to be who you've always been. That's because once they define you conceptually, and learn to relate to you that way, they will resist any changes you try to make. It messes with their routine-way of relating to you.

> To be nobody-but-yourself—
> in a world which is doing its best,
> night and day, to make you everybody else—
> means to fight the hardest battle
> which any human being can fight;
> and never stop fighting.
>
> —E. E. Cummings[23]

Imagine living in a community that insists you are a nervous, clucking chicken. It takes the highest level of commitment to let go of that identity. However, when you commit to genuinely live for yourself, you no longer feel the need to explain yourself to anyone. (Chapter 14 covers this matter extensively.)

THE URGE TO GROW

A fertile redwood seed is conscious of its urge and capacity to grow into a giant redwood tree, and so it does. What about the redwood seed that is not conscious of its capacity? That seed loses the energetic urge, and rots in the soil. What about human beings who are not conscious of their capacity to grow into ever grander expressions of themselves?

The next time you take a stroll on a bright, summer day, bask in the warmth of the sun and feel that *urge* that swells within you. The energy of the sunlight stirs the quickening found in the seed of your authenticity. That's a great moment to ask yourself, "What shall it be, the Maestro or the *intruder* for me?"

The self that sees your future like a big "welcome mat" is the Maestro. When you look at your future from that position you experience yourself as an opening for extraordinary expression.

Then there's the *other self* with all its drama. Only one of these two selves can take root in your mind at a time. Which will you listen to? Ultimately, you decide!

You can learn from what's true, or you can let your false identity burn you. The more conscious you are of what's true, the more you'll find yourself doing what's best for you.

Your eyes are opening:

> The fault, dear Brutus, is not in our stars
> But in ourselves, that we are underlings.
>
> —William Shakespeare, *Julius Caesar*[24]

If it's true that the fault lies not in our stars, but in ourselves when we act like underlings, then it must also be true that the credit lies not in our stars, but in ourselves when we open up to our marvelously made nature and let that flow through.

Let's take a moment to look a little deeper into this matter of consciousness, specifically self-consciousness.

TWO VERY DIFFERENT EXPERIENCES

First of all, you are always self-conscious, meaning *there's always a self at the center of your consciousness of which you are aware.* Survival insists on it. So the important question becomes, "Are you being *awkwardly self-conscious* or *intelligently self-conscious?*"

When you are *awkwardly self-conscious*, you are conscious of your assumptive identity. That identity feeds on uneasy feelings (the *intruder's* favorite meal). Such feelings are the context in which the *intruder* exists!

When you are *intelligently self-conscious,* you are conscious of yourself as the Maestro. With that awareness, you feel inspired and restful, not awkward and stressed.

It's important to note that being *intelligently self-conscious* does *not* mean you *won't* miss the mark. You will miss, plenty. However, you won't feel awkward about it. Instead, you'll see your failures as the ancient Greek archers saw their failures.

THE FINE ART OF SINNING

In Ancient Greece, when an archer missed the mark, it was called "sinning." To sin, back then, had nothing to do with being immoral, unethical, or breaking God's Commandments. It was simply an opportunity to refine your action so you might "win" next time.

We went over this concept earlier with the idea of a *miss-take,* but to be sure it sinks in, I want to offer it again, in a slightly different fashion. When a Greek archer missed the mark, the next logical step was to learn from his error so he could improve his archery skills and try again. Hence the chant of the aspiring marksman was, "Sin and sin until you win."

Were those archers self-conscious? Certainly! However, they were not *awkwardly self-conscious,* they were *intelligently self-conscious.* That's because their interpretation of "sinning" was void of self-condemnation. There was no drama. They were *not* frazzled when they aimed their arrow once again.

Archers of Ancient Greece understood that they had to make changes to their method if they were to improve their archery, and they understood that a calm state of mind would increase their odds of hitting the bullseye the next time.

Children intuitively understand the archers' philosophy about "sinning leading to winning." They naturally know that missing the mark is part of the grand adventure of improving. That kind of sinning stirs their curiosity. That's why children develop so swiftly.

Imagine missing the mark and eagerly saying, "I've sinned, but I intend not to sin again." When you speak of missing the mark as an observation of reality, rather than as a harsh criticism, you awaken the skilled and resilient archer within.

However, when you're feeling *awkwardly self-conscious*, you are standing as the *other self*, judging yourself harshly. And when that's your stance, it's not long before you put your bow away and never pick it up again.

Can you remember a time when you missed the mark, felt awkward, and quit? Would you have felt nearly as awful had you known that missing the mark (sinning), is simply a call for correction? You owe nothing to the *intruder*. You are not required to cooperate with its awkward self-conscious attitude. Agreed?

With this one distinction under your belt, your future failures need no longer hobble your determination. You are more than qualified to be an excellent archer at whatever you set your aim toward. Believe this, and you'll recover quickly, always ready to give it another shot when you miss the bullseye.

Go for it.
Expect to sin!
Expect to win!

Before leaving this chapter, let's take stock of where we are on our journey.

A LONG-LOST FRIEND

Imagine you're traveling all around the world in search of a long-lost friend. You're feeling discouraged, and you wonder if your friend is ever to be found again.

Then, out of nowhere a stranger appears and informs you, "The truth is right in front of you. Yes, you can reconnect with your friend."

He goes on to ask, "Are willing to accept this truth?"

You nod yes, and he says, "Great! You are ready now to discover another vital truth: *help is available.*"

You thank the stranger, and though you are a little uncertain of what just happened, you feel optimistic and energized as you travel on.

All of a sudden, right in front of you, you spot a road sign that reads: *Your Journey Begins When You Travel Within*. It dawns on you: that's the *help available* the stranger was referring to.

Then you exclaim, "Dearie me, I've been looking for my friend, out in the world…in all the wrong places."

Instantly, you turn the direction of your journey inward...and lo, what do you find? That your long-lost friend—the authentic you—has been stuffed in the cargo of your soul every step of your journey.

You feel wonderfully at ease with yourself once again.

Your original nature is your lifelong traveling companion, always as close to you as your awareness allows. When you, once again, embrace your long-lost friend, you realize *nothing* is more refreshing than honest self-investigation. Nothing!

> How wonderfully expansive,
> How neurotically narrow-minded we can be.
> How remarkably swift,
> How terribly sluggish we can be.
>
> The more aware you become
> Of how unaware you've been,
> The wider you open the portal of your mind
> To the truth about yourself.
>
> Remain curious.
> Rejoice in your new awareness.
> Right awareness will set you free
> To know thyself and be thyself absolutely.

Can you see how self-division need not be so difficult to solve? What bountiful blessings might be available if you were to look even deeper into this situation? I assure you what's coming next will give you even more clout to clobber all confusion and doubt.

This is a great time to reveal the specific *cause* of your self-division...

chapter 12

The Tyranny of NO

BEGIN AT THE BEGINNING

While the typical direction of a journey is forward, oftentimes we first need to travel backwards to move forward. Let's go back to when you were born, all the way back to when you were a tiny human being.

As a newborn, your mental slate was clean, you'd written nothing on it: no preferences, no prejudices, no notions about what to expect from yourself or from life. You had no identity. You'd not been told that you were intelligent and talented…or *not*. All you felt was your aliveness, and an inner tug to experience more of that.

The bridge you cross over from a blank mental slate to what's written all over it today—now that's worth examining.

As you began to grow, you quickly became fascinated with language. It seems all of us are language addicts. Language is central to our lives. We just love to learn to talk, and then we love to talk and talk. If we're not talking to someone else, we talk on and on to ourselves.

Our capacity to communicate our thoughts and feelings through language happens quickly, and proves not only to be a remarkable blessing; it can also be a terrible curse. It can help us rise to the top of the toughest mountain; it can cast us into the deepest abyss.

Had you been born in an idyllic Garden of Eden, where only comforting and inspiring words were spoken, you'd have only learned words that supported you.

Unfortunately, that idyllic garden does not exist.
Something happened.

A BOMB WAS TOSSED

You were born into a "world of words," and your mind was a clearing for infinite possibilities, but something happened. During the first few years of adjusting to your new environment—from womb to the living room—a bomb was tossed into your field of consciousness.

That bomb was one of the "first words" you learned—the two-letter word: NO!

We are now getting to the bottom of things, to the source of humanity's primary struggle.

It all begins during the exploratory period in a child's life that we call "the terrible twos." The real question becomes: are "the terrible twos" terrible for the parents or terrible for the child?

Imagine a toddler, two and a half feet tall, running down the hall squealing with delight. He feels the world is wonderful and he senses he's incredible, and he's out to test it! Then, just as he sticks his hand in the toilet bowl, along comes a harsh "NO!"

Every child is born raring to go, however, when his innate curiosity is hit with a NO, how quickly that one word dampens his sense of wonder. Any affinity with the UU quickly fades when those NOs come rolling in.

Wow! This single-syllable word is a bombshell, packed with nervous energy. The child didn't see it coming, and if that's not enough, he hasn't a clue that there are thousands more to come. And as the NOs keep rolling in, the child's deep-seated sense of being marvelously made becomes a distant memory of times past.

As far as I can tell, the word "NO" is inescapable. There's not a culture into which one is born (be it religious, national, social, ethnic or family culture), that doesn't overuse the word "NO."

Unfortunately, children don't have the capacity to judge situations for themselves. Hence they rely on others to inform them, and when the NOs come rumbling in, their unfettered inquisitiveness and unbridled enthusiasm comes to an end.

All NOs cause immediate pain, but it's not the immediate pain, it's the *miss-understandings* that come from the NOs that cause the child lasting discomfort.

A PROGENY OF NO

The *other self* is a progeny of NO. This *self* was not the consequence of a single NO, but rather it was the result of one NO piled atop another. As the NOs continued to flow, fast and furious, carrying psychological wallops like nothing you'd experienced before, you begin to ask the *intruder's* favorite question, *"What's wrong with me?"*

And as you already know, the above question set the footing for your assumptive identity. You created and this entity during childhood moments of hearing hurtful NOs and asking that question.

You gave more and more presence in your life to your assumptive identity, as you became present to more NOs, and began taking them more and more seriously. Those NOs gave you the emotional complexion found in the *poisonality* of your *other self*. In other words, the more the NOs became part of your emotional circuitry, the more muscle you breathed into your assumptive identity.

> Words are powerful.
> Words can shake our souls.
> When NO starts shaking,
> We start quaking.

As mentioned earlier, the word "NO" was installed in human language early on, and hearing highly charged NOs is a fait accompli, an inescapable hazard. You couldn't help but be born into a world that contained a million conversations of NO. Nor can you escape that conversation today. Listen. It's everywhere!

If that weren't bad enough, after being born into a world of NOs, a world of NOs was then born in you, and echoes of NO began howling in the chambers of your mind.

> First, you showed up in the world.
> Then, NO showed up in your world.
> Then the *intruder* showed up in your life.

If you are willing to confront what you're reading right now, fully aware of your power to intervene, soon the walls of NO will come crumbling down.

BUT WATCH OUT!

NOs are the *intruder's* most potent kegs of dynamite. When it tosses one of those kegs into your field of consciousness—kaboom! NO is not only the sparkplug that fires up the *intruder*, it's also the hammer this *self* uses to bang you over the head repeatedly. When left unchecked, the damaging effect of NO can negatively impact you for a lifetime.

Going through the traumatic experience of birth, and then going through traumatic "NO-Experiences" is part of our human-story. Unfortunately, even when a NO is spoken softly, to help a child grow, rarely does the child experience the NO as well-intentioned. Children are innocent. They lack the capacity to understand when a NO is spoken as a loving act. Hence they take all NOs hurtfully.

One moment the child is playfully pulling the cat's tail, and the next moment the guillotine drops: "NO, honey! Don't do that!" Although that NO was well-meaning, the child experiences a feeling of separation—*"I don't fit in!"*

The idea *"I don't fit in"* throws the child into a tailspin. Their feeling of wellbeing thrives when they feel like a member of the tribe. However, when *withdrawal of approval* sets in, the warm feeling of belonging takes a nosedive. The child falls from grace, and not only do they feel separate from the flock, but they also feel constantly watched.

I'm going to be so bold as to say the two-letter word "NO," with its many variations, is the biggest deterrent to humanity's evolution.

BELIEVE IMPOSSIBLE THINGS?

In Lewis Carroll's *Through the Looking-Glass,*[25] a distraught Alice remarks, "There's no use trying.... One can't believe impossible things." I suspect that attitude was a consequence of Alice experiencing her share of NOs in her young lifetime, aye?

Do you remember the White Queen's response? "When I was your age...why, sometimes I've believed as many as six impossible things before breakfast!" I'm guessing the queen was raised in an environment where she was exposed to very few NOs, and if they were spoken, it was very softly.

How else could she have believed in six impossible things before finishing her toast and eggs?

For the most part, the NOs you heard when you were a child are the same NOs your parents heard when they were children, which are the same NOs their parents heard, which are the same NOs you pass on to your children. The NOs of the parents are passed down from generation to generation unless someone puts an end to it.

It has been suggested by some child psychologists that the average six-year-old has experienced 60,000 NOs. I imagine 1,000 NOs would be plenty for a child to come to the decision, *"There's something wrong with me,"* but with 60,000 NOs he comes up with 60,000 different ways of believing that! Even after 500 NOs, why would a child assume the statement, "NO, NO! Don't put that in your mouth!" was meant to be helpful?

When the strong winds of NO come wailing in, they cause a biochemical storm in the child's brain, which adversely affects his physiology and psychology. If it was just the word "NO" that the child stores in his memory, perhaps he could handle it. However, the child comes to another scary conclusion: *"The other shoe is going to drop! What else am I going to do wrong?"*

With fear of the "other shoe dropping," the child wires *NO* and *fear* together, and when that mental circuitry begins firing off in unison—confusion and doubt begin ruling her emotions.

Unfortunately, childhood NOs are not the end of it. NOs gain even more momentum during the pre-teen years, as they take on new forms such as social rejection, mocking, mimicking, and bullying.

By the time children reach their mid-teens, their experiences of harsh correction, rejection, and reprimand give an immense amount of energy to the *intruder.* So much so that it no longer feels like a passing fancy, but like solid reality. That's when teenagers are more interested in playing it safe and protecting themselves than jumping into life and correcting themselves.

And yet, the NOs keep coming still!

All biases and prejudices are forms of NO. With this continual assault of NOs, the brain sends warning signals to the adrenal glands, which release stress hormones that can throw one's entire biochemistry out of harmony, causing digestive disorders, allergies, and even a general weakening of the immune system. The consequences of NO are a big reason why pharmaceutical companies are thriving.

THE NO-STUCK CONDITION

Once a NO takes hold in your psychological system, the *intruder* is like an angry platoon sergeant in your head, barking out *orders to retreat* whenever you're curious about something new. Those *orders to retreat* are a consequence of living with echoing NOs from the past. I call that condition being NO-Stuck.

When you're NO-Stuck, your NOs are howling from years ago, and they howl not once, but repeatedly whenever you consider trying something new. The howl of a NO can be deafening, and what's worse is that the more it howls the more the *intruder* gains control.

> Your fear of failure makes you avoid danger up ahead.
> However, the real danger is rarely up ahead.
> The real danger is the howling NOs in your head.

Have you ever had a throbbing toothache? That discomfort is similar to the nagging ache of insecurity you feel when NO-Stuck. That pulsating ache triggers your fears, which blocks you from accessing your natural enthusiasm for living.

This NO-Stuck condition places us on a slippery slope where we actually begin believing that quitting is an intelligent decision. "Oh, what a tangled web we [unconsciously] weave,"[26] when we unwittingly deceive ourselves into believing we are defective.

Miles Davis once said, "Do not fear mistakes. There are none."[27] When it came to his musical endeavors, he did not let the NOs get to him. He transformed jazz into a whole new art form. Little wonder he's considered a musical genius.

Rather than shaking in the presence of NO, imagine establishing a powerful relationship with it, where you see it as one of the *intruder's* kegs of dynamite, and immediately leap into action to defuse it, like Miles did. Can you do that? Stick with me; you *will* do that!

BUILDING BLOCKS OR STUMBLING BLOCKS?

When you become proficient at distinguishing the truth from the self-sabotaging opinions that come with echoing NOs, your adventures begin! There is no work more important than constructive NO-Work.

I remember watching my niece playing with her wooden building blocks years ago. Tara stacked one block atop the other, and even though they toppled over repeatedly, she didn't quit until all the blocks were stacked neatly.

Why was Tara having so much fun? Because she was not interpreting those tumbling blocks as stumbling blocks. Although the blocks tumbled, her attitude did *not*. She did not berate herself for stumbling. Instead, like the ancient Greek archer, she eagerly refined what she was doing.

Every child has an aptitude for great artistry. Are you *not* one of those children? You're never going to find boots high enough to avoid being muddied by the murky puddles of NO, but disentangling your goals from the morass of old NOs *is* possible!

One way to intervene on a NO-Stuck condition is to begin asking yourself a healthy question that interrupts the usual query, *"What's wrong with me?"* It should be a question that creates space for something new, such as, *"How would I behave if I didn't allow this howling NO to make my decision?"*

When NOs reign, your passion to be curious wanes. Just one healthy question calls forth that passion once again. This single shift in consciousness creates space for you to examine new territory where you've never been.

Fear not, you were born with the capacity to succeed with any building blocks that life hands you, however, if you're to utilize your capacity, it's vital that you see how the *intruder* uses echoing NOs to turn those building blocks into stumbling blocks.

Imagine living, once again, at the level of commitment you experienced as a child, before the NOs crept in. When you set your aim to win with a conviction beyond description, how could an echoing NO possibly throw a monkey wrench into your growth and expansion? It couldn't.

WHAT'S YOUR ACHILLES' HEEL?

Your echoing NOs from your past can come on swiftly and sting horribly. And when the howl of a NO lingers, you feel like you're *not enough*, which is a sure sign of being NO-Stuck.

Is there somewhere in your life where you feel NO-Stuck? When do you think you are *not enough*?

✓ Not smart enough?

✓ Not attractive enough?

✓ Not athletic enough?

✓ Not creative enough?

✓ Not talented enough?

The dispiriting mood that comes with feeling like you're *not enough* creates a great divide between your visions of winning and the decisions you make. Have you noticed? Engage in this conversation so you take it personally.

1. What fantasy of success has become a distant memory?

2. In what part of your life do you endure a troubling condition?

3. Do you play it safe to avoid criticism?

4. Do you aim low for fear of failing?

5. Do you allow others to decide for you for fear of disapproval?

6. Do you avoid intimate relationships for fear of rejection?

7. Do you cower to people in authority?

8. Did you take the time to answer these questions?

Any negative answer are a symptom of being NO-Stuck. There is no vaccine that gives you psychological immunity to this condition, but there are things you can do to strengthen that immune system. We'll get to that, soon enough.

Had you received these words of wisdom about NO long ago, who might you be today? You are receiving these words now. Are you being receptive to them?

We have jumped into the deep ocean of your consciousness. We have begun exploring the depths of your conditioned programming. Perhaps this is the perfect time to get up and stretch? When you come back, bring your diving mask.

We are going to dive deeper, where we find NO's partner in crime…

chapter 13

WOE!

THE MESSINESS OF MISINTERPRETATIONS

I am choosing every word I write in this chapter very carefully, I hope you read it thoughtfully. We're now going to look at another potent keg of dynamite the *intruder* loves to toss into your field of consciousness.

When the mind is spinning in an orbit of howling NOs, it's not long before we feel powerless. It's our misinterpretation of those NOs that justify this weakened condition. The biggest problem that comes with this state of affairs: *we no longer take responsibility for commissioning what happens in our lives.* In fact, we *avoid responsibility* by relinquishing our authority to powers outside of ourselves.

I call this state of affairs: WOE.

WOE is my acronym for, "What On Earth," as in, "What On Earth is doing this to me?"

"What On Earth is doing this to me" is the polar opposite of "responsibility." Unfortunately, when we relinquish our power, we see a harsh world out there, waiting to be documented as proof of why we are so helpless. This emotional state is not natural, it's a learned state where we turn every small incident into a tragedy.

Mark my word: whenever a person continually wails, "WOE is me," that announcement eventually becomes a self-fulfilling prophecy. When you exclaim, "WOE," it's an invitation for life to occur that way for you.

It's strange but true that folks who lament, "WOE is me," vehemently argue their gloomy point of view. They look to get some sort of odd satisfaction from blaming the world for the many injustices they believe they endure. Of course, when one projects outwardly, that kind of energy, most assuredly they will attract more of the same.

When you allow howling NOs to devolve to WOE, you've buried your original nature under a pile of moaning, and you experience yourself *at the effect* of everything. Does this sound familiar? At that point, any feeling of resignation that you may be experiencing quickly devolves to desperation; that's when you begin anticipating more abuses coming your way.

In the mindset of WOE, all our "ways of being" turn into states of fleeing, where we're completely caught up in the role, "poor me." This role is one more tactic the *intruder* uses to grow even stronger. When caught in this orbit of thinking, it's easy to feel cheated and grow bitter as we lament, "I've given so much, and for what!"

There is no opportunity for new possibilities when you are open only to what WOE has to offer.

> Men are born to trouble at first
> and are exercised in it all of their days.
> There is a cry at the beginning of life,
> and a groan at its close.
>
> —William Arnot[28]

Being born into a world of NOs is the first sign of trouble. And once ensnared in the howls of NO, we become exercised in groaning, "WOE," right up until the close of our lives…unless we do something about it.

Get straight with yourself about this. Whenever you wail "WOE is me!" and wallow in self-pity, you refuse to hold yourself accountable for your life. And beware—lamenting WOES will have you clinging to despair, which is like clinging to a bear! Those WOES will rip you to shreds.

You were born in a state of weal,
A vibrant and healthy state of well-being.

Then come the NOs that won't let go.
Then follows the *learned* state of WOE.
That's when self-pity takes its toll.

Indeed, woeful folks are victims,
But not victims of the world.
They are victims of their own ill-operating minds.

Unfortunately, when it goes unchecked, this condition quickly worsens. The moment you open one small portal to let in the feeling of self-pity, you find yourself woefully generalizing about everything.

DISEMPOWERING GENERALIZATIONS

It's simply unavoidable—justifications that support woeful moaning also encourage walloping generalizations. Walloping generalizations are woeful *exaggerations*, where one looks at specific issues and moans on like they are eternal and unchangeable.

When a person woefully generalizes, he points to something "wrong" with the world, with others, or with himself, and then he uses his intelligence to make a universal statement about it. This kind of overemphasis marches his mood deep into the darkness.

A woeful generalization strengthens a defeatist reaction, which in turn strengthens the woeful generalization, which, gives even more strength to the defeatist reaction. It's like a dog chasing its tail; eventually the dog sits down, exhausted and dizzy.

The big problem with woeful generalizations is that they have you *suffer before it's necessary*, and you continue to *suffer far longer than is necessary*.

Here are examples of woeful generalizations:

- There's *nothing* I can do about this problem.
  (*Nothing* is a generalization that stops you dead in your tracks.)
- I'm broke because there are *too* many people and *too* little money.
  (*Too* insists your extreme negative conclusion is an absolute fact.)
- The world is *just not* a happy place to live.
  (*Just* implies there is no other valid point of view.)

- *Everywhere* I look, *everyone* is out to take advantage of me.
  (*Everywhere* and *everyone* block any other possibility.)
- I am *always* breaking things.
  (*Always?*)
- I *never* get *anything* right.
  (*Never?*)

Can you see a link between any woeful generalization you may be holding on to and any moaning you may be entertaining? Can you see how your moaning reinforces your woeful generalization? When you get caught in that trap you eventually sit down, exhausted and dizzy.

How far down the hole can a person go with WOE? This is not trite jargon, it's essential that you understand the clobber WOE carries. WOE is always damaging to your enthusiasm and ambition!

Arnot's opinion that we not only "cry at the beginning" of our lives, but also "groan" at the end is pointing to the fact that if we don't watch out, we can use our power to prove we are powerless for a lifetime!

The first thing we must do, to put an end to being taken over by WOE, is stop insisting we're *always right* about what we claim is *always wrong* in our lives. When we stop insisting that we already know everything is *wrong* in life (negative generalization), we create a little room to see how ineffective the perspective of WOE can be.

The only power WOE ever has over you is the power you grant it. Is that now obvious to you? You grant it power by setting…

WOE-TRAPS

When WOE pounces, it pounces quickly, and it pounces often when WOE-Traps are set in your field of consciousness. The bait that ensnares, is a falsehood, cleverly disguised as the truth. An example of such bait would be the answer you get from asking unhealthy questions, such as "What's wrong with me?" or "How can I be so unlucky?"

> Then, SNAP!
> That's the clamping sound of a WOE-Trap.
> Once WOE has you, you're caught in your "poor me" act.

I guess a man is the only kind of varmint

sets his own trap,

baits it,

and then steps in it.

—John Steinbeck[29]

Only *you* can set a WOE-Trap in your field of consciousness, and only *you* can step in it. You know when a WOE-Trap snaps; you feel the sting of falling back. Your mind's madness inevitably attracts badness, which delivers sadness.

Hear the good news! You can dismantle your WOE-Traps. The first step to doing that is learn about the kind of bait you use to set them. Here are more samples of unhealthy questions that are WOE-Trap bait:

- Why is life so unfair?
- Why me, Lord?
- What have I done to deserve this?
- Why don't I get any breaks?

To dismantle a WOE-Trap, you simply need to *flip* the unhealthy question. For example, flip "How can I be so unlucky?" to "How many ways have I been lucky today?" This one simple flip expands your perspective to recognize favor where before you only saw fault.

Sound too simple?

It works if you mean it to work.

When knocking on the door for healthy answers, knock persistently. Tomorrow's answers are planted with today's inquiries, but you must seek them purposefully. Truth loves the persistent inquirer.

You need not take orders from WOE.

You have the right to say "No" to WOE.

Stop loving the idea of being helpless.

Start loving the idea of being helpful.

From helpless to helpful,

Healthy questions are the vehicle.

Certainly, there will be times when feeling a little woeful seems unavoidable, like when the weather is awful, and the concert is canceled. However, on such occasions there is still a healthy question available: "What might be the blessing I'm not seeing in this situation?"

Is there any negative generalization that may be stopping you from appreciating this conversation? Self-correction is always a matter of facing that which is self-effacing. As you already know, one major purpose of this book is to help you lose self-effacing delusions so you can embrace the truth of your extraordinary nature.

Life never leaves you with just one road to travel. Lamenting WOEs lead you down bumpy roads. Healthy questions support healthy feelings, which turn your life in new directions. Those feelings are signals—you're on the road to healing.

Our only real enemy has always been *our ignorance* of our marvelously made nature. When you believe in yourself, you attend to yourself. Make the UU a thought-habit, and before you know it there will be you and a life of infinite possibilities, with nothing in between—no NOs and no WOES to delude you.

FACE IT

Whenever you start wailing WOE, it's a psychological blow. Refuse to compromise with the truth any longer. You are not here to *endure* life; you are here to *enjoy* life!

When it feels like you are just enduring life, look into what you are wrongly presupposing, be it about a relationship, a money issue, or a job promotion.

At first, you may not see a connection between your relationship problem and a woeful point of view, but if you persist, it won't be long before you say, "Oh, I see something about myself I didn't see before." What you see is the *miss-understanding* and the false justification you've been using for your continual moaning.

Woeful moaning, backed by false justification, is akin to a tranquilizer being shot into the heart of your passion—with each moan causing your mood to plummet lower and lower.

When you are on the go with WOE, you are going *nowhere*, and you die without knowing the true reason why you are here.

Here's another way to look at the ill effects of WOE: Imagine strapping a heavy sack of hay onto the back of a leopard. He's bursting with speed and talent, but with that extra weight, he just can't get up and go! Woeful moaning straps heavy sacks of howling NOs on the back of your soaring spirit. Once this happens, you've given your thinking over to the woeful *intruder*, completely.

> Life's but a walking shadow, a poor player
> That struts and frets his hour upon the stage
> And then is heard no more: it is a tale
> Told by an idiot, full of sound and fury,
> Signifying nothing.
>
> —William Shakespeare, *Macbeth*[30]

Someone with persistent money issues struts and frets about a *lack* of money. He is most definitely correct that there is *lack*, however, the problem is not his *lack of money* as much as it is his inner *feeling of lack*. The odds are he's listening to a howling NO around money that began years ago, causing him to moan a thousand times since then.

Living with NO and WOE is like walking through a minefield in your mind, where the moment you step on old NO—*Kaboom*—there's an explosion of moaning WOES! Whenever the NOs howl inwardly, you moan outwardly, it all occurs quite mechanically.

Shakespeare also refers to this condition of continual moaning with the statement found in *Julius Caesar*: "A coward dies a thousand times before his death, but the valiant tastes of death but once."[31] The coward jumps back to old NO-Scenes repeatedly, which begins his ritual of woeful moaning continually. The valiant person experiences the NO but once, learns a valuable lesson from it, and moves on.

> Hear ye! Hear ye!
> WOE is a gigantic hoax!
>
> When WOE rules your life, NO runs your life.
> When NO runs your life, WOE ruins your life.
>
> It's time to stop living with self-deceit.
> It's time to stop accepting self-defeat.

Self-deceit and self-defeat compel you to retreat.
That's when anxiety sets in and the moaning restrengthens.

If you want to fly higher you've got to think higher.
That's what sets your ambition on fire!

Can you give me one valid reason for you to allow lamenting WOES to run through the streets of your mind like an angry mob? Foolish question, right? Let not a single woeful moan compromise the truth about your ability to make your dreams of yesterday your reality today.

> You see things; and you say, Why?
> But I dream things that never were;
> and I say, Why not?
>
> —George Bernard Shaw, *Back to Methuselah*[32]

It's your turn to say, "Why not?" Saying "Why not?" continuously gives you supreme advantage over the *intruder* with his lamenting WOES.

KICK THE LEGS OUT

There's a way to neutralize your woeful generalizations by kicking the legs out from under them. The "legs" are the rationalizations and justifications supporting those erroneous points of view.

Let's look at the woeful generalization: "I *never* get *anything* right." Wait a minute, can that possibly be true? We are coachable when we are open to new ways of looking at things.

> Student: "I *never* get *anything* right. I don't know what to do?"
> Teacher: "List the many things you do get right, like driving your car, texting on your phone, or making yourself a nice cup of coffee, then come back."
> (One week later)
> Student: "Here's my list, it's pretty darn long."
> Teacher: "By making a list and looking at it, you've already loosened the grip that woeful generalization had on you. Awareness is the first step."

You can serve only one state of mind at a time. Choose WOE, and you've chosen a state of mind that puts you in decline. When "WOE is me" is the *cause*, feeling helpless is the *effect*. And when you're feeling inwardly woeful, being outwardly reliable is impossible. A great step toward correcting that attitude is to unceasingly embrace the Critical Addendum to the UU.

Let's look at the facts according to the Critical Addendum: when we set our mind to doom and gloom, and begin whining to prove we're right… we do "win" at what we've set our mind to—*whining*! And when we "win at whining" we set ourselves up for "winning at losing." It can be no other way. If you want to start "winning at winning" you've got to stop whining.

> The unexamined life is not worth living.
>
> —Socrates[33]

The biggest problem with unexamined WOES is that you take the mood with you wherever you go, and every minor bump becomes a major blow. Furthermore, you're living in an unpardonable state where even if you do achieve something of value, it never feels like enough.

> NO and WOE grow like fungus.
> They thrive best in damp, dark, emotional environments.
>
> NO depends on WOE to keep its echoes audible.
> WOE depends on NO to keep its mood substantial.
>
> When it comes to mental malpractice,
> NO and WOE are on the "Most Wanted List."

The more WOE and NO grow, the less you grow. Also, the farther back in time your WOES go, the deeper the blow. That's when your historic WOES no longer lie in your past, but start driving your future.

> If only NO had *not* struck like a rattlesnake,
> And WOE had *not* squeezed you like a python!
>
> When caught in the role of the helpless victim,
> You see your life as an unfillable hole.
>
> Oh, so quickly you dial back your goals,
> And tell yourself, "I'll never feel whole."

It's time to reclaim your power. The groans about which Arnot wrote are *not* writ in stone. You can withhold your power from the forces of NO by no longer being a cheerleader for WOE.

What would it be like to be *rightly sensitive* when WOE has captured your attention? When *rightly sensitive*, you become suspicious at how skilled you are at playing the role of "helpless victim.'"

And with old woes new wail my dear time's waste.

—William Shakespeare[34]

Your world occurs as frightful when you allow WOES to frighten you, however, when you handle those WOES effectively, you waste no time with new wails, and if you do, those wails are frail at best.

In this chapter you've learned to engage in the *act of subtraction*, by ridding yourself of false justifications for validating WOE. When you *subtract* like that it becomes apparent that there's nothing you need to *add* in order to claim your inherent position as the Maestro. It's all right there!

As we continue our travels through the dark valley toward the sunny meadow, I will continue to alert you to booby traps, so you don't fall back. There's a little more thicket we need to cut through, but your machete is sharper now, and the going gets easier.

Oftentimes, the first step to embracing the truth simply requires removing oneself from the wrong crowd...

chapter 14

Be Ye an Eagle or a Crow?

THE IMPACT OF CONVERSATIONS

In many social circles today, it's a popular pastime to involve oneself in conversations that have us "seeing through a glass darkly." It's not unusual to find folks engaged in "yada, yada" that begins with moaning and ends with groaning.

When you participate in a community where feeling discordant is commonplace, all your happy memories and dreams of a promising future are buried under a big pile of WOES. That's because folks in that community ship in the WOES by the truckload. If they're not promoting negative platitudes and expressing defeatist attitudes, they're engaging in *fore-bemoaned moaning* (another great Shakespearean expression) where they bring yesterday's WOES to life once again.

> The eagle never lost so much time
> as when he submitted to learn of the crow.
>
> —William Blake[35]

Cawing crows are a gathering of folks caught in the victim role: victims of the weather, victims of a recession, victims of the government, victims of foul play, victims of circumstances. You name it, they are victims of it, and they want you to know it. Furthermore, they are constantly on the lookout to validate their WOES.

When coming from "poor me," no one speaks from right-reasoning, but rather from disgruntling emotions: "The humidity was unbearable.... The food was terrible.... The traffic was miserable.... My date was disagreeable.... I paid too much for my new car.... I didn't get enough for my old car.... I missed the concert and was terribly upset.... I went to the concert and was terribly bored."

Woeful chatter puts everyone in a trance of troubled conformity where even the mention of the Ultimate Understanding sounds like foolish fantasy. What's worse is that it takes but one champion of complaining— one cawing crow—to get the whole room cawing.

CAW, CAW, CAW

When folks of that feather flock together, a defeatist attitude builds as everyone piles their unique version of, "WOE is me" on top of the last one. With a whole room of folks cawing, and everyone chiming in, it's not long before the conversation snowballs out of control. One woeful tale piggybacking upon another, adding more and more links of stress to the chain of upsets until an attitude of relentless gloom inevitably takes over the room.

> Rocky and slippery is the trail when cawing crows reign supreme. The lamenting thoughts that come with cawing are blind and lame guides.
> Cawing crows are expert at stirring up cantankerous inner contemplation.
> Cawing crows are expert at stirring up outer displays of exasperation.

A cherished hobby of lamenters of WOE, is collecting past disappointments to validate their negative generalizations. They use their disappointments as evidence to prove, not only how tough life is, but to predict how bleak life will be.

The *"need to fit in"* is a prevailing craving that keeps a community of woeful moaners together. They will say anything to feel like they are part of the flock. Pretty soon a pattern of noble suffering sets in, as they all self-righteous, piously lament in harmony, "Life is hell, and the best we can do is endure it."

How can you possibly share anything of any value when you're in a room full of folks sharing projections of gloom? You can't! That's because from their perspective nothing is going to work, and whatever lingers longest in a person's consciousness shows itself strongest in his life. Oh, what a price we pay when we use our minds the wrong way!

It's a darn shame how contagious a gloomy mood can be when "WOE" is repeated over time. Soon it becomes a toxic routine of the mind, and you can be sure that any "high" one gets from lamenting WOE, will be nothing more than an emotional cocktail that leaves him with a wicked mood-hangover.

And heaven forbid anyone should try to cheer up a flock of cawing crows for any reason. If one member of the flock shows the slightest sign of strength by offering a *counter to cawing*, oh, how quickly the others lash back about how insensitive that person is.

Back in the 1930s, many cattle farmers would wrap the twine used for bundling hay into a ball, which would grow huge over time. Some farmers took great pride in this hobby. Frank Stoeber, of Cawker City, Kansas, had a ball of twine that weighed over 5,000 lbs. He donated it to the city. Next thing you knew, many more folks were adding more twine to the ball. Guess what it weighs now? Over 19,000 lbs.!

How many generations have been adding "whine" to humanity's swirling ball of woeful cawing? If it was weighable, I suspect it would be as heavy as the planet. Little wonder so many folks are WOE-Stuck. Have *you* added any "whine" to that ball?

If you removed the "woeful twine of whine" from the nesting ground of cawing crows, do you know what you'd find? What was standing there before the WOES began: a roomful of human beings brimming with talent and optimism.

NESTING GROUNDS

Where, in your neighborhood, might you find nesting grounds for cawing crows (folks who love gathering in the name of talking about what's unfair)? Oftentimes, all you need do is frequent a local coffee shop, nail salon, bingo parlor, barber shop, or tavern, and there's a good chance you'll hear some cawing.

There is absolutely nothing of any value to be gained from being a member of a cawing crow social circle. What good can possibly come from sacrificing one's natural sense of optimism and ambition for the applause of others? Whenever you allow others to use your mind as their caterwauling playground, you've handed your life over to the *intruder*.

Is it possible there are social gatherings in the name of joyful harmony? Are there nesting grounds where folks engage in conversations that begin with, *"You think that's good, listen to this"?* You're darn tootin' there are! We live in a world of contrariety; how else can it be?

If there's a world of "WOE" then, logically, there has to be a world of "WOW." Cawing crows find others crows to caw with. Soaring eagles find other eagles to soar with. When you make your life an expression of gratitude and appreciation, cawing crows avoid you no matter where you go.

I'm not saying you should strive to live in a community that is absolutely WOE-free. Clearly, you cannot avoid living *in* a world where there are cawing crows, but the messages they offer need not be the platform from which you launch your thoughts.

Suppose you refuse to use WOE to start your conversations anymore? Suppose you refuse to walk into work with woeful tale on your mind? It's not your social responsibility to participate in conversations that energize woeful whining. If you find yourself caught in such activity, the first thing to do is take responsibility for being part of it. Sometimes breaking from the flock, and flying solo for a while, is a necessary first step to catching your breath.

It's not only sensible to break away if cawing crows invite you to play, it's downright practical. Here are some suggestions to help you avoid getting caught in WOE-begotten cawing.

THREE TIPS

TIP # 1

When folks gather in the name of complaining and *fore-bemoaned moaning*, imagine yourself sitting in the bleachers, passively watching a marching band that's stumbling around the playing field. You notice they're all playing their instruments out of tune.

One thing you most definitely do *not* want to do is react by howling back. Have you ever watched a video of South American howler monkeys jumping up and down on the branches of a tree? Their howling is quite a comical scene and a useless expenditure of perfectly good energy. You are far more evolved than that!

Don't add to their lamenting by judging them. To do that is to fall into your own WOE-Trap, and your deed will then rebound with like-kind impact (like a ball tossed against a wall). For example, if you complain about their groaning, you'll further agitate their already ruffled feathers and they will most certainly lash back with greater ferocity.

You've heard the phrase, "turn the other cheek," haven't you? Well in this case, you must turn your thoughts in the opposite direction from what they are offering and walk to a place of peace in your mind. You're seeking what Wordsworth called, "the landscape with the quiet of the sky."[36] That's where higher wisdom exists.

TIP # 2

The only power cawing crows have over you is the power you grant them. You do yourself a world of good when you understand the true nature of goodness. Consider it a crime of the mind to grant their moaning any valuable time in your field of consciousness.

When you find yourself at a cawing crow festival, close your eyes and imagine you're standing in the calm eye of a hurricane with howling winds all around you. Then send out your own currents of calming energy. Simply smile pleasantly. It has to begin with someone; why not you?

TIP # 3

There's no doubt about it; sometime today or tomorrow someone will approach you with a conversation of WOE. Consider it a hot potato and drop the dang thing before it burns you! Often, you'll find this vision is all you need to interrupt the pattern and change the tone of the conversation. Remember: right consciousness always offers right responses.

THE TRUTH IS OUT

We've pulled back the curtain! WOEs are like hungry pigeons gobbling up breadcrumbs in the park. Your WOES are your *intruder's* pigeons, gobbling up your visions of joyful living. Anytime you see WOE for what it is, you are able to reclaim a little more of your power and offer a healthy response that shoos away all woeful thoughts that give sustenance to moaning.

> Two men look out the same prison bars;
> one sees mud and the other stars.
>
> —Attributed to Frederick Langbridge[37]

The reason a person would see mud is because of woeful self-deception. The reason a person would see stars is because of healthy self-perception. Amazing possibilities present themselves when you rightly say, "Enough is enough already, and I am plenty enough already."

- ✓ Plenty smart enough already
- ✓ Plenty talented enough already
- ✓ Plenty resilient enough already
- ✓ Plenty capable enough already
- ✓ Plenty creative enough already
- ✓ Plenty flexible enough already

Knowing that you are "plenty enough already" attracts a new awareness. You find yourself in an impressive position when you get beyond your WOE-Conditioning. However, until you take responsibility for the possibilities that exist beyond your WOES, there are no possibilities beyond the limits that your WOES impose.

If you're to hold yourself accountable for experiencing all of your *enoughness*, so you can see all the stars that are available, it's wise to be your own porter.

CHECK ALL LUGGAGE

Imagine boarding a train with a lot of heavy luggage, and while hauling your baggage, you stumble and fall.

> A porter asks, "Why are you hauling so much luggage?"
> You argue, "It's all mine, and every bit of it is necessary for my journey."

The porter points out, "You're accepting fiction as fact. It is not all yours."

You insist, "All of it belongs to me."

The porter replies, "Look at the luggage tags."

You check the tags and realize that much of the baggage belongs to passengers you've met long ago on your life journey.

Now I ask you, "How much excess mental baggage are you carrying? What woeful thought-voices do you assume belong to you? What negative judgments and opinions belong to cawing crows from your past?"

It's time to be your own porter.

Remain alert.

Whenever you're feeling bogged down with excess baggage, slow down and ask yourself, "Where did this thought-voice originate?" That one question will lighten up your mood. When you lighten up, you light up. That's because you find plenty of room for the enlightening truth to travel with you.

If there have been any bumps in the road we've traveled to this point, I hope I've helped you drive around them or float over them. The next chapter is a lot of fun. It explains how to travel smoothly, no matter what the road looks like.

Prepare yourself for some powerful practices on how to intelligently address NO-Dramas that cause WOE-Traumas, so you can quickly reverse that curse. We learn best in a state of joy. Do you have a genuine smile on your face?

Good. Let's go…

chapter 15

Vital NO & WOE Gauges

THE DASHBOARD OF YOUR PSYCHOLOGICAL SYSTEM

The gullible are unaware of their gullibility. The ignorant are unaware of their ignorance. You are no longer gullible, and you are no longer ignorant. A quote attributed to the Chinese philosopher Lao-Tzu says, "If you do not change direction, you may end up where you are heading." So, now the question becomes: Will you drive through life responsibly so you end up where you want to go, or will you allow the *intruder* to do the driving?

If you're going to travel the high road of life, with the Maestro behind the wheel, it's important that you learn about the NO & WOE Gauges.

One might assume a car's mechanical system and a human psychological system have nothing in common. Well, surprise! They both have gauges (indicator lights), to alert us when problems arise.

It's obvious, when planning an auto trip you must pay attention to the gauges on the dashboard of the car (the speedometer, voltmeter, oil gauge, and temperature gauge). That's how you avoid driving with a rattling engine and steam blowing out of the radiator.

Yet how many folks, when planning their journey through life, ignore the NO & WOE Gauges on the dashboard of their psychological system? We don't usually subject our NOs and WOES to analysis; we simply take them for granted. Well the truth of the matter is that when a NO-Gauge is blinking, it's an indicator, alerting you that your nervous system is overheating. It's important that you make a correction. That's how you avoid traveling through life with a rattling mind and steam blowing out of your ears.

If you ingested toxins, you'd go to any length to rid your body of them, wouldn't you? Why treat your mind any differently? If you intend for your life journey to be a smooth, you must cleanse your mind of toxic moods brought on by NO and WOE.

The NO & WOE Gauges tell you when you are in high tension "overdrive," so you can change gears. They also signal when you are running on automatic and heading in the direction you don't want to go.

If you know what to do when these warning gauges are blinking, you have the technology to manipulate your neurology so your life-trek is a piece of cake instead of rife with emotional aches.

Let's look at your NO & WOE gauges so you can put the Maestro back in the driver's seat.

NO-GAUGE #1: LOOK AND KNOW...OR...NO-GO

This gauge indicates your approach to life:

- Look and Know is a winning approach.
- NO-Go is a whining approach.

Whenever you set a goal, there comes a moment when you commit or restrict. The decision you make determines your success or failure rate.

OPTION #1: LOOK AND KNOW

Look and Know is when you *look* at the future *knowing* you can achieve your goal.

When you *Look and Know,* you may be fanciful-hearted when you begin, but you're fact-minded before you are done. From this perspective your sight is clear, your vision *feeeels* real, your plans are specific, and your action is direct.

In this ambitious state, you seek solutions continually, and you fill your day with practical steps, knowing they will lead you to the ultimate prize you envision. This is a winning way of being in life.

However, you have another option.

OPTION #2: NO-GO

NO-Go is when you look at your goals and nervously say, "NO, I can't possibly go there."

A *NO-Go* outlook is fraught with doubt. When this is your decision, you are *not* receptive to hearing solutions. You're slicing out a piece of life that could have been very rewarding. The best that can come from this position are brief moments of wishful thinking followed by briefer moments of unproductive action.

How do you know when the *NO-Go* gauge is blinking? Your stomach rumbles, your heart palpitates, your language is ambiguous, and you are adept at excuse-making.

INDICATOR LIGHT: YOUR MOOD

- A superior mood indicates you're looking at your goal from *Look and Know.*
- An inferior mood indicates you are looking at your goal from *NO-Go.*

Either you're on the path to committed action…or you're not. If you're not, you're sensing something's wrong. What's wrong is the howling NO followed by a rancid WOE.

MAKING CORRECTIONS

Life's challenges are meant to prod you to grow. *Look and Know* is the way you grow. However, when the indicator blinks *NO-Go,* a mood adjustment is called for.

You always have the capacity to transform an inferior mood into a superior mood. Here's one way to do that: recall a time when you successfully accomplished a goal from the mood of *Look and Know.* You did what was needed, and you succeeded. Remember? You were in that mood when you were learning to read and write, swim, and ride a bike. Jump into a memory of sweet success with the intention of embracing that mood once again, then ask yourself these four questions:

1. What bodily sensations did that superior mood give me?
2. What did I say to myself?

139

3. What color would I pick to represent that mood?

4. What size container would I need to pour that mood into?

If you've experienced that superior mood once, you can experience it again. All you need to do is deliberately drop yourself into that memory and allow its victorious feeling to overcome you once more.

NO-GAUGE #2: ROBUST CURIOSITY...OR...NO-IT-ALL

This gauge indicates your psychological state:

- Robust Curiosity has you inventive and attentive.
- NO-It-All has you weary and defensive.

Challenges can fall upon you like hailstones from a bright, summery sky—rattling your state of mind. In such moments there's a choice to make.

OPTION #1: ROBUST CURIOSITY

Robust Curiosity is an astute state of alertness where you focus your attention only on answers.

When robustly curious, you're eager to inquire into what you must do to succeed. That's when you respond to life without your old NOs and WOES handcuffing you.

Curiosity, when directed effectively, transforms any feelings of self-deficiency into a strengthening feeling of self-sufficiency. This opens you to resources that you've been ignoring.

However, you have another option.

OPTION #2: NO-IT-ALL

When "NO!" reigns, *NO-It-All* is your psychological game, and your curiosity wanes.

From the perspective of *NO-It-All,* you insist you know all there is to know, hence, you arrogantly say, "NO," to any new suggestions, which guarantees that your unrealized potential will remain unrealized. This mind frame creates an enormous chasm between the life you live and the life you yearn.

A horse trainer once told me that no matter how much time he spent domesticating a wild horse, it never lost the yearning to run free. He explained that a penned-in wild horse senses the wide gap between the life it is living and the life it craves...and sadly you can see it in the horse's eyes.

When your mind is penned in with NOs, you have tunnel vision and your stubbornness shows in your eyes. This mindset restrains you from seeing anything but the limited options you're already looking at.

However, there's a big difference between a human being who's penned in with a *NO-It-All* mind-frame and a horse that's penned in—a horse does not have the capacity to open the gate and set itself free.

When you say, "NO" from a *NO-It-All* disposition, you are more concerned with protecting your current limiting decisions than opening the gate by looking into things more deeply.

> Nothing can work me damage except myself;
> the harm that I sustain
> I carry about with me,
> and never am a real sufferer
> except by my own fault.

—Attributed to St. Bernard of Clairvaux[38]

Oh, yes! *NO-It-All* takes its toll! Expecting inspiration from a *NO-It-All* position is as foolish as expecting warm sunshine from a blizzard.

INDICATOR LIGHT: YOUR INCLINATION

- With *Robust Curiosity* you are cool-headed and open-minded.
- With a *NO-It-All* frame of mind you are uptight and hellbent on being right.

MAKING CORRECTIONS

If you're to correct a *NO-It-All* disposition, you must value inquisitiveness more than taking everything so personally. That single shift in consciousness creates space for you to examine unexplored territory. It takes but one healthy question to call forth your passion for learning once again.

If you're willing to build just a small bridge between what you stubbornly insist is true and what reality is telling you, such moments can be remarkable opportunities for healing stubborn resistances. This gauge is alerting you to that.

WOE-GAUGE #3: FLOW...OR... WOE-ATTACKS

This gauge indicates your temperament setting:

- Living in Flow has you harmoniously on the go.
- Living with WOE-Attacks has you flailing in the flood waters of WOE.

What's the temperament of the scenes you project on your mental screen? What do they project? Do they have you gently rowing your boat down the stream of life, do they have you reactively thrashing while paddling?

OPTION #1: LIVING IN FLOW

When *Living in Flow* you strike a timbre of YES when you conjure a vision of success that you intend to manifest.

The experience of flow adds a sense of certainty to your intention, which augments your level of efficiency. You look at your desired outcome like you have *already* achieved your goal, even though you know you haven't, and that confidence guides you to accurate decisions when it's time to initiate action.

However, you have another option.

OPTION #2: WOE-ATTACKS

A *WOE-Attack* is a like a purse snatch, but what's snatched is your determination.

When a WOE attacks and you fearfully react, what's being snatched is far more valuable than the contents of any purse. You've given up control for feeling helpless. What kind of life can you have when the feeling of helplessness is in control? That, right there, is a capital crime of the mind!

WOE-Attacks are as unpredictable as crazed cats. Watch out—they do scratch!

INDICATOR LIGHT: YOUR CONSTITUTION

- Your constitution is cool-headed when you're *Living in Flow*.
- Your constitution is faint-hearted when you experience a *WOE-Attack*.

MAKING CORRECTIONS

You conquer a *WOE-Attack* by daring to look right through the fearful feeling of helplessness that comes with it. When you take the time to investigate, you find it's nothing more than a past woeful memory that has been triggered by something happening right now. The howling NO, behind the WOE, is insisting you *re-act* in the same dramatic fashion you acted back then.

Imagine you're walking by a police station and you hear a police car siren blaring. You notice an officer rushing to the car and you ask, "What's happening?"

The officer gasps, "We're reacting to something that happened years ago."

"That's crazy," you respond. "Have you temporarily lost your sanity?"

Isn't that what's happening when you react to an echoing NO, from years ago, provoking a *WOE-Attack*? The threat is imaginary! Have you not temporarily lost your sanity? Understanding the insanity of reacting to yesterday's WOES is a sign of spiritual maturity.

The last thing you want to do when experiencing a *WOE-Attack* is to stare at it frightfully. What you stare at stares right back, and that intensifies the energy of the attack. Prefer simplicity. Choose the truth of your marvelously made nature over the intimidating message that WOE offers. Never listen to WOE like it's intelligent.

True guidance requires being levelheaded so that productive orderliness may once again settle over your mind. That's when you see the pointless pain you're putting yourself through. A wailing WOE may feel powerful, but its discouraging report is revocable. That attitude alone is a powerful WOE-Stopper. Is this an oversimplification?

No, it's a simple truth.

A perfect follow-up, after stopping a *WOE-Attack*, is to take a moment to do something that's productive. It need not be complicated, simply something that feels reassuring and constructive. Perhaps you simply clean off your desk. Doing something useful, by itself can be an effective pattern interrupter.

By the way, if you are sneering at these ideas right now—what *is* that? Is it possibly a *WOE-Attack*? This is yet another opportunity to expose the mechanics of your assumptive identity with its many woeful tendencies. Does that sound unreasonable? Be unreasonable—it works!

NO-GAUGE #4: YES-LOOP...OR...NO-LOOP

This gauge indicates the nature of your self-talk:

- A YES-Loop is inner narrative that's encouraging.
- A NO-Loop is inner narrative that's discouraging.

Your mind works in a circular fashion, spinning and spinning, continually looping back to the initiating thought. The mind just loves folding back on itself, coming up with like-kind thoughts to reinforce prior thoughts that support your first thought.

It often takes a simple understanding like this one to replace self-treason with right-reasoning. When you commit to addressing what's rendering you powerless, with an eye for improvement, right-reasoning comes naturally.

You have a choice to make when engaging in self-talk: you can do so encouragingly, which conjures scenes of victory that have you feeling enthusiastic and ambitious, or you can play reruns of old NO-Videos that give you the jitters.

Which choice will you make?

OPTION #1: YES-LOOP

When you support a *YES-Loop,* you give your mind a positive spin.

Your first thought is encouraging, and you consciously spin your self-talk upwardly from there. The energy is inspiring. This circular chatter motivates you to reach higher.

Example of a *YES-Loop:* Imagine your original thought is, "I wonder if I should start my own business?" Now the mind starts spinning. "YES, being my own boss is something that excites me. YES, this is going to be a lot of fun. YES, I have what it takes to start my own business and make a lot of money."

In a *YES-Loop,* your mind's natural tendency is to circle back around to the original thought and come up with even more ideas that fortify that idea. You feel confident and competent as you formulate a concrete action plan, which drives you to jump in and get started.

However, you have another option.

OPTION #2: NO-LOOP

When your self-talk supports a *NO-Loop*, your mind is caught in a negative spin.

It's impossible to create anything new when your inner dialogue has you replaying old NO-Tapes. That discouraging conversation is like a committee of nay-saying thought-voices in your head, telling you what's wrong with you and anything you're thinking about. The *NO-Loop* is now on a roll. The demoralizing tone of those thought-voices attracts mental scenes of failure and loss, as they pile one problematic supposition atop another.

Your negative self-talk spirals your circular thinking ever downward, and your mind chatters on with lame excuses and unfounded reasons why you cannot win, which further talks you out of ever giving your ambitious ideas a try.

Example of a *NO-Loop*: Imagine the same original thought as above: "I wonder if I should start my own business?" However, now comes a discouraging thought-voice: "Start my own business? Am I crazy? NO, NO, NO. Who do I think I am? I'm going to lose my shirt!" And down you go.

This discouraging spin demolishes your dream. You imagine yourself having to sell your car just to pay off your new debt. And what does the mind do next? It circles back around with a dozen more discouraging opinions that reinforce the downward spin, blurring your vision of success even more.

Just as a dark cloud covers the bright sun, a *NO-Loop* covers your bright enthusiasm by giving you 1,000 contradictions that empower discouraging feelings. In order to escape that feeling, you quit before you begin.

INDICATOR LIGHT: TONE OF YOUR SELF-TALK

- Your inner tone of voice is lilting when you experience a *YES-Loop*.
- Your inner tone of voice is distressing when you experience a *NO-Loop*.

MAKING CORRECTIONS

When the *NO-Loop* gauge is blinking, you are riding a string of Nervous Nellie thoughts, however, you need not abdicate your power. This is a perfect opportunity to call upon your Power of Intervention.

You can pull the circuitry on a *NO-Loop* by disconnecting its pattern of circular thinking. You do that by disassembling it and examining its individual parts. And the best time to do that is when the *NO-Loop* is in full swing. Begin by asking yourself these questions:

1. What am I saying to myself?
2. What tone of voice am I using?
3. What discouraging opinion am I repeating?
4. What mood am I generating?
5. What's my facial expression?

You are the master electrician when it comes to your mental circuitry. You are always capable of wiring a new string of strengthening opinions into your nervous system until they fire off together. You do that by simply standing tall and purposefully adding a positive spin to your thinking. It's simply a matter of stating the opposite of what you were saying, and doing so with an encouraging tone of voice.

You can weaken any *NO-Loop* the moment you become aware of its working parts by immediately intervening with encouraging opinions and keeping it up until those opinions feel unquestionably true for you. It's always uplifting when you sweep away the sandy soil on which a NO-Loop stands, so you can stand on solid ground and start building what you're seeking. (More details on how to do this in later chapters.)

Converting *NO-Loops* to *YES-Loops* is healthy therapy. It can clarify your visions of winning in all domains of living, be it with your relationship, your spiritual growth, losing 30 pounds, or starting your own business.

There is one more gauge to look at.

NO-GAUGE #5: CANNOT...OR...CAN-NOT

This gauge indicates your temperament when making decisions:

- "Cannot" is a responsible response—a result of logical thinking.
- "Can-NOT" is an aggressive response—a result of feeling defensive.

Whenever you size up a challenge you are also sizing yourself up. You do that by unconsciously asking, "Can I handle it?" If you feel you cannot handle it, there is something you want to look into.

OPTION #1: CANNOT

"Cannot" is the conclusion you come to only after investigating the matter sensibly.

If it's not possible to do what is being asked of you, then it's intelligent to say, "I *cannot* handle it." Certainly, there are things you simply *cannot* do. For example: "I *cannot* fly a Lockheed Martin F-22 Raptor fighter plane."

However, sometimes there are things we *could* do if we really tried, but we select the other option.

OPTION #2: CAN-NOT

"Can-NOT" is to look at a challenge irrationally and *insist*, "I can-NOT do it, no matter what."

When you turn the word "NOT" into a verb, as in *"can-NOT,"* it is very revealing—there's a howling NO making your decision, and your emphasis is on the NOT. You are reacting defensively. You're being very stingy with yourself. You're not putting yourself out there. Emphasizing the word NOT, is a way of saying, "I will do whatever it takes to prove it is *impossible* for me to do this."

For example: when it comes to losing weight, is it really valid to say, "I cannot lose weight"? Or are you stubbornly insisting, "I *can-NOT* lose weight!" In the latter case, what you're really saying is, "I *will* NOT lose weight—I *won't!*" From that stubborn conviction, you commit to NOT losing weight by having a piece of cake.

When folks place themselves on the side of, "NOT doing something that is doable," there is no budging them. Imagine what would happen if they put themselves on the side of doing it with that same conviction!

INDICATOR LIGHT: YOUR APPROACH

- Your approach is level-headed when you legitimately say, "I *cannot.*"
- Your approach is emotional and obstinate when you insist, "I *can-NOT.*"

MAKING CORRECTIONS

When the *can-NOT* gauge is blinking, the grimace on your face is very telling. It projects stubborn inflexibility. Consequently, you are *miss-using* your "power of will" by insisting you are helpless in a situation where you are not.

Imagine a child insisting, "I *can-NOT* read…I *can-NOT* write…I *can-NOT* swim…I *can-NOT* ride a bike." Holy moly, what a pickle that child would put himself in!

Whenever you bull-headedly insist, "*I can-NOT*," there's only one thing holding you back—*you!* Hard to swallow? If someone says, "I *can-NOT* spell," what are they really saying? They are insisting they most definitely will NOT put in the effort to learn how to spell. The can-NOT sounds deceptively intelligent, but it's uncompromising stubbornness. By the way, there's no such a thing as a bad spelling gene.

So, what to do?

What task in your life right now do you insist you *can-NOT* handle?

> I *can-NOT* stop smoking.
> I *can-NOT* get along with my neighbor.
> I *can-NOT* help but get angry when I'm around my son.

Ask yourself, "Is it possible that my *can-NOT* is an arrogant statement posing as an intelligent one?" Just asking this healthy question creates space to look at the situation again. Now comes the opportunity to think from the truth of the matter, not from your emotions.

I bet the list of things you truly cannot do is a lot smaller than the list of things you claim you *can-NOT* do. What do you think?

INTELLIGENCE OR EMOTIONS?

Although we like to believe it's our intelligence that determines our decisions, for the most part it's our emotions that govern them. When we're stuck in the past because of howling NOs, our lamenting WOES override any intelligent decision. Oh, how we waste our talents and strengths when we refuse to look at the NO & WOE Gauges!

In the next chapter I am going to tell you a few short stories that give examples of folks who successfully let go of the tyranny of past NOs—*or didn't*. I ask that you look at yourself, inside the stories, and notice what they may reveal to you about yourself…

chapter 16

Personal Stories of Letting Go

ROB

This story is about me and a can-NOT. When I was a kid, I took trumpet lessons from a crotchety instructor, who told me, "Some people have 'the chops,' but you're *not* one of them, Bobby." Well, given he was an expert (I thought), and given I was naïve, I took his NO seriously. I immediately came to a self-limiting decision: "I can-NOT improve much with the trumpet; I do not have the chops."

Despite my can-NOT, I was persistent with my lessons, but unfortunately, I'd unconsciously decided the best I could ever achieve was *mediocrity*. Consequently, I endured with my trumpeting endeavors long enough to become a so-so musician. Occasionally, while in my early 20s, I'd played with a small band, but that was it for me. I can see now that, when it came to my trumpet-playing journey, I never stopped listening to that howling NO.

Were you waiting for a happy ending? Sorry, this happened years before I learned what I'm now sharing. Remember the Critical Addendum to the UU: we are destined to win at whatever we set our minds to. I proved it!

However, there is a little more to the story. In every adversity lies the seed of a remarkable lesson. In my mid-twenties I had the good fortune of meeting Miles Davis, the acclaimed jazz trumpeter. During our brief conversation, I told Miles I loved the trumpet but just didn't have the chops. He looked at me and laughed. After a moment of awkward silence (awkward for me), he said, "If you've got lips, you've got chops. You've got to put in the time to develop them."

What?

Could that be true?

Miles taught me something I've never forgotten. I was absolutely certain that a problem existed that *didn't*, and I'd set my mind to proving it… and I did. The opinion, "I do *not* have the chops," and the decision, "I can-NOT play well, no matter how much I practice," became a strong but wrong opinion that I refused to violate.

After my encounter with Miles, I realized I'd been duped, *not* by my trumpet instructor, but by *myself*. Ah, the power of the mind! Can you think of a can-NOT you've bought into? Truth can be painful, but it can also be wonderfully freeing.

Now, onto folks who did break through NO and WOE to something fresh and new.

KAREN

Karen would wake up every morning, swirling in self-talk about how unyielding the world can be and how powerless she was in the face of life. Her narrative contained a litany of NO-Loops, and she gobbled them up like breakfast Froot Loops.

When Karen spoke with me about her morning ritual, it was clear she was a specialist at assuming the worst. For example: she couldn't sleep for days when her cat got sick; that's because she'd convinced herself Muffy was going to die. She explained to me that her woeful mood got the best of her, so much so that she ended up with a terrible cold from the worry. That was several years ago. Muffy is still alive today! Thank goodness Muffy didn't buy into Karen's NO-Loop.

I described the movement of a NO-Loop to Karen and explained how we develop strong relationships with the things we hope won't happen, because we grant those thoughts prime-time in our mind.

I suggested Karen *do nothing* when she was caught in such a loop of thoughts. I went on to explain what I meant by *doing nothing*. It's not that you surrender to the NO-Loop, but rather, you listen to it for what it truly is—meaningless mind-chatter. Further, I explained to Karen that looking at the meaninglessness of her NO-Loops will never lead her astray, but instead, will create a clearing so she can intervene in an effective way.

Karen began listening to her NO-Loops with the intention of ridding herself of them. As she began to objectively analyze the different elements of her NO-Loops, she saw how easy it was for her to rationalize her feelings of impending gloom without any real evidence or facts. She could also see how her rationalizations helped her add even more gloomy thoughts to her NO-Loop. That's when she came to realize that the only power her NO-Loops had in her life was the power she granted them.

Shortly thereafter, Karen became skilled at flipping NO-Loops into YES-Loops. She loved the results she got, and so with that victory under her belt, she became proficient at converting NO-Go into Look and Know.

With awareness of the NO-Loop and the NO-Go Gauges, Karen went on to make two remarkable changes in her life: she went to couples counseling with her husband to work out some ongoing problems, and she opened a yarn shop with her sister—a dream they had shared since high school.

Not too shabby, wouldn't you say?

JIM

Jim was convinced he was born a nervous wreck, and there was nothing he could do about it. When Jim and I first met, he exclaimed, "As long as I can remember, I'd shake all over when I tried something new." I wanted Jim to understand that his nervous reactions were not genetic imprints, but rather were the consequence of WOE-Attacks.

After several conversations, Jim finally agreed to look deeper into his nervousness, and to remain open to its root cause. With his new curiosity, Jim began to see himself in new ways. The idea of WOE-Attacks intrigued him, so much so that he committed to putting an end to his wailing WOES.

One day, out of the blue, Jim went to a local toy store and bought a cheap tin sheriff's badge. He began carrying the badge in his pocket to remind himself *he* was the sheriff in town when it came to his attitude. And no longer was he giving his authority away to *fore-bemoaned moaning*.

That's when the fun began!

When Jim felt on edge, he'd take the badge out of his pocket and pin it on his shirt. He didn't care where he was or who he was with. Then he'd quietly say to himself, "I'm the new sheriff in town, and my job is to enforce the law. The law is clear: WOE-Attacks are outlawed." That one statement was a great pattern-interrupter for him.

Jim didn't stop there; he came up with six healthy questions he memorized for just such occasions. Or, as he likes to put it, "I keep my mental six-shooter loaded, and I'm not afraid to use it."

Here are Jim's questions:

1. What's happening right now that's setting me up for a WOE-Attack?
2. What *miss-understanding* am I accepting that has me feeling helpless?
3. If I look beyond my usual reactions, what possibilities might be open to me?
4. What should I remember about myself that empowers me?
5. What quality of character should I call upon to strengthen me?
6. What action can I take right now to exercise that quality?

With his badge and these six questions, Jim began tackling his attacking WOES before they gained momentum. He found his questions were what created the space he needed to deal with his WOE-Attacks.

It has been less than a year since Jim began wearing his badge, and he feels he'll be able to retire it soon. Ask Jim about his victory, and he'll tell you, "Nothing stops a WOE-Attack like understanding what it is and where it's coming from."

STEVE

One of Steve's favorite things to do is daydream. For years, his most-visited daydream was about owning a corner store. Yet, whenever the time came to act on his dream, his programmed mind would churn out a multitude of nay-saying thoughts until, inevitably, he'd adopt a NO-Go attitude.

However, it didn't end there. After Steve's NO-Go attitude settled in, a can-NOT would come rumbling behind it, like thunder: "I can-NOT possibly make that happen." Then a NO-Loop would pitch in: "How dumb can I be? That's a stupid idea. Leave well enough alone. I should be happy I've got a decent job."

Steve's NO-Go... can-NOT... and NO-Loop would decimate his motivation. At most, he would make a feeble attempt to move toward his dream, but he'd give up the instant there was the slightest resistance.

When I explained to Steve about the two selves he was dealing with: the resourceful and capable self, and the *other self*, he laughed heartily. But soon thereafter, he began asking questions. That's when I introduced him to the NO-Gauges, and showed him how to use them. He loved what he was learning, and grew fiery and excited about making changes.

Steve began consciously creating YES-Loops that led to a successful coup. The *other self* was on the run! Steve's battle cry went like this:

"YES, if I can conceive of owning a corner store then I can achieve it."

"YES, I have what it takes."

"YES, I've learned valuable lessons from my failures in the past."

"YES, I will now put those lessons to good use."

It was but 18 months after setting himself loose from the tyranny of his NO-Go and can-NOT attitude, that he purchased a corner store and named it "Steve's Place." Yes, it's actually on a corner! Six months after purchasing the store, Steve was doing well enough to buy a van and offer free delivery service to local customers.

It doesn't end there. He is now pursuing his PPL (small plane Private Pilot's License), yet another can-NOT he's converted into, "YES, I can."

A SCORPION'S DESTINY

I imagine you've heard the story of the scorpion and the frog? A scorpion asks a frog for a ride across a pond. However, first he has to convince the frog he won't sting him while crossing.

The scorpion explains, "If I sting and paralyze you, I too will drown. I cannot swim. How stupid would that be?"

Seems reasonable enough, right?

The scorpion jumps on the frog's back and off they go. Yup, you guessed it. They barely get halfway across the pond when the scorpion stings the frog.

The frog, now paralyzed and gasping for air, manages to wheeze out, "Why did you do that? We're both going to die!"

The scorpion gulps, "I'm a scorpion. Stinging is what I do. It's my destiny. I couldn't help myself!"

Well now, on the other hand, *you*—unlike the scorpion—are a free agent!

You have plenty of options!

So, what stinging habits are you clinging to that are killing you? What can-NOT...or...what NO-It-All has you splashing and panicking? If you're drowning in a sea of regrets, you now know who the scorpion is that is stinging you with those habits—the *intruder*!

Does this story, or any of the above stories, remind you of a time when you redefined yourself, and changed your behavior to achieve something new? Can you recollect the wonderful feeling that came with that correction?

With your new awareness you can become a mighty conqueror of any *miss-understandings* that give life to the *intruder* and his stinging habits.

I'll complete this chapter with an old movie scene I'll never forget

A FLARE GUN

The movie opened with novice campers hovering over a fire, frightened by howling wolves. The howling went on for hours into the night. The next morning, a seasoned trailblazer happened to pass by.

After listening to their story, he gave them a flare gun and some flares, and explained, "If you shoot the flares into the sky, the howling wolves will run away to avoid being exposed by the light."

Sure enough, the wolves returned the following night and began howling. The campers shot a flare into the sky, and the wolves quickly fled in fear of the light.

Consider me a trailblazer.

I've handed you some flares.

You don't have to be super-talented or super-intelligent to rid yourself of howling NOs or lamenting WOES that are dwelling in the caverns of your consciousness. However, you do have to pay attention to the NO & WOE gauges if you're to handle them effectively.

When you catch a gauge blinking, pay attention. Be responsible and ask yourself, "What NO or WOE do I have to deal with right now?

- NO-Go?
- NO-It-All?
- WOE-Attack?
- NO-Loop?
- can-NOT?

In the future, when the howl of that old NO or the lament of an old WOE summons a discouraging scene on your mental screen—consider that scene a dumb rental. Return it to the archives from whence it came and pledge never to rent it again. There—you have yet another flare.

We're not done—there is a magnificent flare yet to come!

However, now that I've mentioned "archives," what better moment than now to look at *your* story…

chapter 17

Reframing Your Story

GETTING PERSONAL

Perhaps you're tired of hearing me say this, "You've got to get personal with this stuff if it's to have an impact on you." Well, you do. Are you ready to take a look at your personal narrative, your story? After all, that is one thing that is *totally yours*.

Your story is your psychological memory of what happened to you. It is your emotional explanation of what went down. You bring that story with you wherever you go. To create a future *not* given to you by your past requires that you study your story carefully, with an eye for how much your past influences you. When you do that, there's something very interesting you'll notice:

- There's what actually happened—the facts.
- There's your interpretation—your judgments, explanations, and all the meanings you gave to the facts.

The interpretations and explanations you gave to the facts become your memory. And your judgements about all of that comes from the understandings and *miss-understandings* you came to about yourself back then.

Problems arises when you take the facts of a NO-Chapter and mingle them with a woeful interpretation. That's because what actually happened (the facts), devolves into drama, and drama only serves the *intruder's* notion of "poor me." Worse yet, you're now stuck with that frame of mind until you interpret that NO-Chapter differently.

The way out of that trap is to begin seeing the difference between the facts of those NO-Chapters and your stories about them. It's your elaborations of those NO-Chapter that heavily influence your report on "why you are the way you are today" as well as your thoughts on "who you'll be tomorrow."

It's relevant to realize that when you're stuck with howling NOs from NO-Chapters, you're stuck with the *intruder's* frame of mind. Furthermore, when you're stuck with the *intruder's* mindset, you cannot notice anything new that you did not notice back then. And that's when your interpretations of those howling NOs are no longer in the past, behind you, they are now continually calling you to react again like you did back then.

When you are caught in the above predicament, you no longer have your past, but your past has you, which means you're being run by what *was,* rather than intelligently preparing for *what's next.* That's what it is to be literally stuck in the past. Your past NO-Chapters are literally making your decisions for you. Folks who feel they have no future are caught in this quagmire, and are blinded from seeing new possibilities.

Can you see the price you pay when your inner narrative is about past NO-Chapters?

LETTING GO

Imagine setting up a very different relationship with your NO-Chapters, so instead of being in the world with those chapters hindering you, you are in the world with those same chapters helping you. That would be you taking responsibility for your experiences of those chapters. Powerful! Do you know what it takes to do that? It requires a total flip of attitude by asking, "What can I learn from those chapters?"

A great way to learn from your NO-Chapters is to take a close look at the *miss-understandings* you came to back then. If you've misinterpreted even one of your NO-Chapters to *mean,* "I am not worthy of a great life," and you reference that chapter today, you can bet you'll go through your day feeling the same insecure way you felt back then.

A paramount reason for learning from your NO-Chapters is to loosen the negative grip they have on you. Do you know what happens if you take the time to give *new meaning* to what happened in such chapters? I'm *not* talking about changing the facts, just changing the meaning you tagged to the facts. In such moments, you rewrite your past. Now the world occurs for you differently, which leads to openings for new action today.

Again, I emphasize that giving *new meaning* to the chapter is not adding or subtracting facts to what happened, but rather, it's reinterpreting the facts of what happened so they empower you.

Please understand, I am not trying to make you "not be" the way you are, but rather, I want to help you open your eyes to the way you *truly are*, and help you understand the reasons why you are not experiencing your marvelously made self as you truly are.

We attain freedom as we let go of whatever does not reflect our magnificence.

> A bird cannot fly high or far with a stone tied to its back.
> But release the impediment, and we are free to soar to
> unprecedented heights.
>
> —Alan Cohen[39]

Any disempowering interpretation that you've given to a past NO-Chapter is a *stone* tied to your back. The burdensome emotion accompanying your interpretation is the impediment that is stopping you from soaring to unprecedented heights today.

Let's not forget that you are marvelously made and destined to win at whatever you set your mind to. Stop fleeing that reality. It's time to let go of the impediments that say, "NO" to your dreams of tomorrow.

Hear ye the great news:

- You can penetrate old myths and misinterpretations you hold of yourself.
- You can reinterpret the facts of your NO-Chapters.
- You can give them new meanings that lead to empowering "ways of being."

The work you're doing right now empowers you to free yourself of old interpretations of NO-Chapters that set your mind to floundering rather than soaring. It doesn't serve you to regret your past. When you do that, you infect your present consciousness with the same discouraging attitudes you had back then.

Any NO-Chapter that you're still compulsive about will affect you differently when you see it differently. When you take the time to reflect on your past with the intention of giving new meaning to those nasty NO-Chapters, you create a clearing to notice positive aspects of yourself you didn't notice back then.

IT'S NOT FATE

You need no longer feel stuck on a wheel of fate that places your past in the future. When you reinterpret your NO-Chapters you step off the wheel. And with your old meanings behind you, it's easy to add inspiring chapters to your future that please you.

There is a process found in all chapters of your story.

- There's the actual facts of the incident—what happened.
- There's your explanation of the incident—your interpretation of what happened.
- There's your experience of the incident—that comes from your interpretation.

Now you know the truth—your experience of an event comes from your explanation of what happened, *not* from just the facts themselves. The facts are always the facts, waiting to be interpreted by you.

With the above in mind, what if you were to look back at a NO-Chapter that is still adversely affecting you, and consider it from a new perspective?

What if you were to extract an empowering lesson from that chapter, which would give the incident new meaning? What might be your experience of that chapter now?

What if you were to squarely face what happened in the NO-Chapter, but this time looked with an attitude of intrigue rather than alarm? Just, what if?

One of the peculiarities of being human is *our insistence on being right*. We will fight and fight to prove we're right. Oh, how we love to be right, no matter what the cost may be. Imagine letting go of insisting you're right with your current explanation of a past NO-Chapter?

You are a very powerful person. You choose your experience in every circumstance. It's not "what happens" but the meaning you give to "what happens" that determines your experience. The meanings you give to the facts are always far more important than the facts. *Nothing, nothing, nothing in your life has any meaning until you give it meaning.* Hard to believe but true.

Are you willing to look at one of your NO-Chapters with real inquisitiveness so you may rescue yourself from your disempowering iterations about that chapter? Again, you're not avoiding facts; you're simply go to give new meaning to the facts.

It can be a breakthrough moment when you recognize those poisonous snakes that *you* have placed on the road of your past. Are they really poisonous snakes? What if you transformed them into harmless udon noodles?

Any time you reinterpret a past NO-Chapter to your benefit, you transform a poisonous snake into an udon noodle, and by doing that, you extract yourself a little more from your assumptive identity. That alone will triple your efficiency when scripting your future chapters, so they delight and excite you.

LET'S DIVE IN

Okay, let's find a NO-Chapter in your story that is still adversely affecting you. Let's begin by having you consider yourself *wrongly serious* about the meaning you gave that chapter. You are being *wrongly serious* whenever you muddy the fact that you are marvelously made, no matter what happens to you. That's seriously wrong to do.

The weak become strong when they see where they were *wrongly serious* and take the time to make it right. That's what this is about.

> …There is nothing unclean of itself:
> but to him that esteemeth anything to be unclean,
> to him it is unclean.
>
> —Romans 14:14 (KJV)

You make the truth of your good and beautiful nature *unclean* when you consider yourself flawed, and are serious about that. When you take responsibility for deeming unclean what is clean about you, and when you get *rightly seriously* about correcting that error—what a difference that moment makes. Ready to take the plunge?

FIVE-STEP REINTERPRETATION PROCESS

Step 1: Choose a chapter in from your autobiography with a howling NO in it.

Step 2: Take a moment now to sit comfortably and watch that NO-Scene on your mental screen. But this time watch it like you're watching someone else's story. Simply look at the what happened without any interpretation. Don't allow yourself to emotionally react.

Step 3: It's time to reinterpret what happened by asking yourself:

- What *miss-understanding* was influencing my interpretation of that scene back then?
- What can the facts of that incident teach me now, that I did not notice back then?
- How can I reinterpret the facts in a way that strengthens me?

Step 4: Review that NO-Chapter again with your new interpretation in mind. Rejoice in the feeling of having just formed a new opinion of yourself. Why *not* live with the highest opinions of yourself? There's no reason not to!

Step 5: Look at the new meaning you gave that NO-Chapter once again. Now that you know that it's *not what happens* that truly matters, but the *meaning* you give to what happens—can you feel your power surging from within?

How'd you do? You did the exercise, didn't you? With all that you've learned about yourself and those howling NOs, how did you use this knowledge to clean up what was unclean for you? Perhaps you have to go through the process again.

You've got all you need to extract a powerful lesson from any incident in your past. Be innovative, use all the information you've assembled from the prior chapters.

If you feel you need a little more clarity on how to effectively apply the *Five-Step Reinterpretation Process* to that NO-Chapter, perhaps the story about Jason will help.

JASON

Jason was a teenager who had many run-ins with the law. When I began working with him, I asked him to tell me about himself. I found his interpretations of his NO-Chapters alarming. There were two particularly strong but wrong conclusions he'd come to, which were very damaging to his self-esteem and his future:

1. "Everybody's *always* up my ass about everything I do."
2. "There's *nothing special* about me; I got no talent and no brains."

Wow! How's that for toxic generalizations! When I suggested that his opinions were reckless crimes of his mind, he laughed and called me crazy. I went on to explain that it was his interpretations of his NO-Chapters that were causing him a lot of misery.

He glared at me and retorted, "What are you, one of those motivational people who thinks they can save everyone?"

I calmly responded, "No, but I do think if you turn to your own resources, you can rescue yourself from a lot of your bitterness."

Jason was a perfect example of someone who was *wrongly serious* about the meanings he gave his NO-Chapters. Little wonder the idea of a productive and happy life sounded like a bad joke to him.

"Yes, reinterpreting your NO-Chapters is possible," I told him. "You don't have to distort the facts; it's a matter of giving new meaning to what actually did happened. When you do that, you'll be able to experience your past in remarkably new ways that can change the way you see yourself today."

We spoke about this over several weeks before he was willing to look at his NO-Chapters in a new light. It was a huge breakthrough for Jason to learn that he didn't have to assume the worst about himself. He began to see how the events that occurred in his NO-Chapters were not nearly as harmful as were the wrong interpretations he'd given them.

I vividly remember the moment when Jason caught on that his opinions about himself were seriously wrong, and it was "those opinions" that were flawed—not him! That's when we began putting some serious time into giving new meaning to his past.

Shortly thereafter, Jason showed up with a list of bad habits he'd developed from his misinterpretation of old NO-Chapters:

- ✓ I'm quick to think the worst when things go wrong.
- ✓ I'm quick to feel like an outcast when I make a mistake.
- ✓ I'm quick to turn a small incident into a big fight.
- ✓ I'm quick to quit when things get tough.
- ✓ I'm quick to blow up when someone corrects me.

After reading the list to me, Jason laughed and said, "Damn! Those really *are* crimes of the mind." We both laughed hysterically! He then looked me straight in the eye and said, "Crimes of the mind, crimes in the street. Crime doesn't pay." I was blown away. Oh, how his smile brightened with his new, elevated self-esteem!

Jason reinterpreted one specific NO-Chapter in a way that was life-changing for him. His father had come home drunk one night, slammed the front door, gone into Jason's bedroom, and called him a worthless bastard. He then banged Jason around before stomping back out of the apartment. Jason had not seen his father since.

Those were the facts.

When Jason first brought up this memory, he was not able to talk about it without feeling angry and bitter. As we worked together, the facts of the story didn't change but his interpretation surely did. He was able to recall the incident in detail without adding any harsh judgment or bitter remarks.

That's when Jason could see that his father had serious problems of his own to deal with. He could see how his father had acted destructively out of his own painful past. "My God," Jason said. "My dad thought of *himself* as a worthless bastard, not me!"

Here's the real prize that came from this breakthrough moment for Jason: not only did he let go of thinking he was worthless, but he went out of his way to find his father, who he'd not seen for years. They've met several times since then and are working at improving their relationship.

Reinterpreting that one NO-Chapter made an astounding difference in how Jason feels about himself in the world today. He feels compassion for people he once hated, and he has attracted many new friends into his life.

Jason will tell you, "It's the tough stuff on the inside I had to deal with before I could stop being a tough guy on the outside."

Oh, and did I tell you—Jason is now in his junior year at a state university!

There are millions of marvelous human beings who are stuck with impoverished models of reality, which are a consequence of being *wrongly serious* about their interpretations of their past NO-Chapters. Hear this! That condition need not be permanent. Jason proved that.

WHO'S DOING THIS TO YOU?

The next time you feel like you're on the edge of a cliff because of a howling NO, take a moment to ask yourself, "Who placed me here?"

And the next time you feel like you're getting pushed off that cliff, take a moment to ask, "Who's pushing?"

The only person who can place you there, and the only person who can push you off—is YOU. And you do that by being *wrongly serious* about howling NOs from past NO-Chapters. That's just wrong! Take that seriously.

Why not float above the edge of the cliff? Why not raise your level of awareness to the Ultimate Understanding? Is that permissible? That is permissible! A great aid to doing that is to extract empowering lessons from all those NOs in your history.

Why enjoy sniffing just one rose in your garden when an entire garden of roses is available? The more you look back with the intention of finding "the rose" in a NO-Chapter, the more you smell the entire bouquet of wonderful fragrances emanating from your entire autobiography.

The next time you sniff a foul-smelling opinion you hold about yourself, pause to ask, "In what chapter of my autobiography did this opinion originate?" Now take that incident through the *Reinterpretation Process.*

Truth invites you back into its circle, but only on its terms. In the presence of truth, you can do everything you cannot do in the presence of error. It's always healthy to inquire into your past with the intention of correcting your *miss-understandings.* You move closer to a world of love and laughter every time you do that.

What storms have you caused yourself to bear?
What dreams have you ensnared in your NO-Net?
What visions have you *not* given wings to?
What toxic spears have you pierced through your enthusiasm?
What misjudgments have turned you from a believer to a doubter?

Certainly, you will err and will continue to make errors…but you, most definitely, are *not* an error. You are a rich and majestic child of infinite intelligence!

A commitment to a great life includes committing to draw on all the lessons that both your NO-Chapters and YES-Chapters offer. If you keep going with this, soon you'll find there are no NO-Chapters, just YES-Chapters! That's when all the chapters in your story offer you powerful references for living a life of love and laughter.

We have reached a compelling point in our journey. Once you fully grasp what's stopping you from understanding yourself correctly, it's easy to get to know the authentic "I AM" you've been waking up with and going to bed with every day since birth…but lost sight of, long ago.

There can be no more spiritual or practical purpose in life than to be true to the true you. So hang on…you are about to step into Part Three of this journey and meet…

PART THREE

high spirits as you are revealed

chapter 18

The Maestro

JUST WHO DO YOU THINK YOU ARE?

This is where you recall what you'd forgotten about yourself. We've spent a good deal of time exposing the *intruder* and its many dirty tricks. That was necessary so you could free yourself to express yourself in ways you've always wanted to.

Here's the ultimate truth, when it comes to you and your life: you are the *Maestro*!

The Maestro is your perpetual selfhood in its undefinable essence. Your highest guidance comes from this source. At this level of consciousness, *you* are the wizard, the ace, the ninja, the composer of your many worldly destinies.

The Maestro is not an acculturated phenomenon, it is a consciousness beyond any conditioned state of being. You are not taught to be the Maestro, this state of being exists beyond your mind. Hence you experience the Maestro directly when you take resolute ownership of your life.

The more you feel at home with your authentic nature, the more you'll experience yourself as the Maestro. When you occur to yourself this way, you enjoy displaying the eminence of your infinite intelligence.

Considering yourself "the Maestro" might have sounded foolish before you began dismantling those *miss-understandings* you've been holding on to for so long. But now, with the knowledge you've gathered and the insights you've had, you are much more aware of the "I" that knows you, when you *know* that *you* know that "I."

> There was a young man who said, "Though,
> It seems that I know that I know,
> What I'd like to see
> Is the I that knows me
> When I *know* that I know that I know."
>
> —Alan W. Watts[40]

In that profound state of knowing, you are in a fluid, unsinkable, resplendent and transcendent state of being, which makes it obvious: "I am a rich and majestic child of infinite intelligence, and am as creative as the cosmos." Furthermore, you hold yourself fully responsible for conducting your affairs and orchestrating the unfolding of your life.

So, how does your currently programmed mind, with its conditioned ways of reasoning, make sense of this truth? It doesn't. That mind, for the most part, belongs to the *intruder*, who wants nothing to do with the truth about you.

A GRAND SYMPHONY

If you consider life to be a grand cosmic symphony, then when it comes to *your part*, you are not only the player, but also the composer and the conductor. As the Maestro, you are fully cognizant of that, and you love adding sweet melodies that define a little more of the undefinable you. Furthermore, you know that without *you*, something is missing in the grand cosmic concert.

> Your life is your unfolding symphony.
> Your unfolding symphony is yours entirely.
> When the Maestro composes your master composition,
> Your commitment is to the highest quality of expansion.

When you accept that you are the Maestro, your metamorphosis from your assumptive identity to the Ultimate understanding is unavoidable.

Welcoming yourself as the Maestro grants you access to exceptional qualities such as…

DOUBLE-EDGED AWARENESS

The Maestro's double-edged awareness is your aptitude to observe your *conditioned awareness* from the sovereign position of *unconditioned awareness*. Whenever you look at yourself from this perspective, you are not in the least blinded by limiting decisions, impeded by faulty conclusions, or hindered by erroneous beliefs that come with those *miss-understandings* you're still holding on to. Only then can you realize the truth that comes with seeing clearly through eyes that are free from myths and superstitions about you.

Your conditioned awareness is the *intruder*.

Your unconditioned awareness is Self as Maestro.

Your double-edged awareness gives you a double-edged advantage over the *intruder*, because you see the disadvantages you've imposed on yourself with your conditioned awareness, which frees you to live from the power of your imagination rather than past programming.

It's with your double-edged awareness that you're able to step off the treadmill of your daily grind and rise above your "nay-saying" programmed chatter, so you can replace old "I AMs" with new ones. Immediately you see through the thousands of nagging trivialities, which leaves you standing tall, with poise, balance, and equanimity in the face of any adversity.

How sweet it can be when you're aware of your NO-Conditioned personality (the *poisonality* of the *intruder*), and are no longer affected by it. That's when your emancipation from your assumptive identity happens systematically. No more veils of lies covering your eyes. You objectively see the insanity of the *intruder's* subjective reasoning, and consequently, it has no control over you.

Having double-edged awareness also gives you double-edged leverage over your challenges because in this state of elevated awareness, you never ever permit discouraging thought-voices to make decisions for you.

As you can see, with the Maestro governing your day, every day becomes *pay day*. Your natural effort, as the Maestro, has an entirely different feel than the anxious effort of the *other self*. That's because you not only hold yourself accountable for composing your own symphony, but you also love contributing to the unfolding composition of all humanity.

UNMATCHED POTENTIAL

As a newborn, you inherently knew your potential was unmatched in the face of any challenge. That was you, as the Maestro, looking at your new world with intense curiosity, and seeing nothing but vast possibilities.

As you grew, Self as Maestro claimed many "I AMs" that gave you expansive expressions of many talents of which you now excel at. It's the Maestro that turned your challenging moments into stepping-stones to grander heights of expression, ever moving you toward other things you could excel at.

You are at a momentous point on this journey. You now know how you came to retire your position as "the Maestro" and allowed the *great pretender* to take over. Furthermore, you now know that inching along through life as a crawling caterpillar or transforming into a high-flying butterfly is never a matter of random chance, it's up to you. You are a rich and majestic child of infinite intelligence, you are the boss's child, you are the Maestro, you decide!

Even in those many, many moments when you've been unconscious of self as Maestro—the Maestro is always conscious of you. Experiencing this truth has come and gone, come and gone—like dancing and stumbling, and then dancing once again. Can you sense that?

If you're entertaining any thoughts about the Maestro being a myth, you know which self is commanding your attention.

Are you ready to claim the truth?

I am the Maestro.
I compose, orchestrate, and conduct my worldly affairs.
I am the Maestro.

By claiming this truth you are embracing the *self of all selves*, the *self* that never has forsaken you. Abandon your old logic. Cast aside your usual ways of thinking about yourself, and right there... feel that! That's you— the Maestro!

Don't consider the Maestro your silent partner, for that idea implies separation. You are the Maestro, through and through. The Maestro is you. Too simple? You want it more complicated than that?

As the Maestro you already know there is no virtue you yearn to express that you do not already possess, and you know all there is to know about your rich immensity because you are *all that.*

> Your life is life's gift to you.
> Life is a miracle.
> You are a gift to life.
> You are a miracle.

Be prepared to reveal the secrets of your heart to yourself as you welcome back the Maestro. You'll glow as you show your beautiful virtues in spontaneous ways, unrestricted by memories of who you mistakenly thought you were.

Would you like to know a great way to experience yourself as the Maestro? Greet everyone you meet with the respect you would give Toscanini, that brilliant Italian conductor who led many of the world's greatest orchestras. What you recognize in others you inevitably recognize in yourself; it's simply a matter of honest projection. It's also the Golden Rule at its highest application.

What better way could there possibly be to experience yourself as the Maestro than to turn the golden rule into a golden tool by respecting everyone as a Maestros—each orchestrating their divine verse, perfectly blending with the sublime wholeness of the universe.

When you see others this way, you slip into a rapturous state of non-judgmental union with everyone, and any walls of separation you've built between you and others come tumbling down. Sweet glory. That's when you realize that what you do for others, you are doing for yourself.

YOUR BONA FIDE POSITION

Now that you're letting go of your burdensome ways of being, it's time to step up your game. There is no healthier thing you can do for yourself than to consider the Maestro your innermost position of absolute authority, enabling you to mold yourself into a jewel of sheer beauty: translucent, resplendent, utterly breathtaking. An inner world of power and action exists, and you have access to it when you accept truths such as this.

The truth will never lead you astray; it will always lead you the right way, no matter how much you've denied it in the past. Your life need not be held together by fearful thoughts. By acknowledging yourself as *the maker* as well as *the made*, as the one who has claimed and experienced thousands of "I AMs" in your lifetime— you are declaring yourself master of yourself.

No man is free who is not a master of himself.

—Epictetus[41]

There is so much more of you to joyfully express than you can possibly fathom in this moment. Today and tomorrow you will conceive and experience many more "I AMs." No time is better than now to embrace the Maestro and claim mastery over yourself with no escape clause.

Over 2,000 years ago, it was written:

For unto everyone that hath shall be given,
and they shall have abundance.
—Matthew 25:29 (KJV)[42]

Are you not one of the *everyone that hath*? You shall be given an abundance of wealth in every realm of life when you see yourself that way. That is the way of the Maestro.

Imagine sitting peacefully on a warm spring day, in the cool shade of a blossoming cherry tree, appreciating yourself as the Maestro, blazing a path toward rich self-fulfillment, in a fashion where no opposition can stop you.

Fantasize rushing home on a brisk fall day to escape the cold of an early winter storm, appreciating that same feeling. What's to stop you from living your life that way, every day, no matter what season of the year it may be? Nothing, other than the *intruder*, can stop you.

To continue with the same text from Matthew:

But whosoever that hath *not*, from him shall be
taken away even that which he hath.
—Matthew 25:29 (KJV)[43]

The *intruder* is where the feeling of "hath *not*" comes from. In that state, even the few memories of glory you've managed to stockpile slip away, be it while sitting in the shade of a blossoming cherry tree or when escaping the cold of an early winter storm.

> Hear ye, hear ye!
> Your heart beats in the Maestro's heart.
> The Maestro's heart beats in your heart.
> You are one heart.
> There is no separation.
> Question not what you are hearing.
> Simply feel your heart beating.

It's time to confirm your inherent position as the Maestro, again. Improvise and even dance while chanting the words. Have fun with this. There is no wrong way of declaring, "I am the Maestro." The purpose is to let The Maestro vibrate through every atom of every cell of your body.

Ready!

> *I am the Maestro.*
> *I orchestrate and conduct my worldly affairs.*
> *I am the Maestro.*

Feeeel that. Let it overwhelm you. From the darkness created by the *intruder,* you grow, once again, into your magnificence. Do you have a mirror handy? Look into it. Give yourself a big smile. Now say, "Yes, I see you in there." Look deep into your eyes and notice who's looking back.

SAIL OFF THE EDGE

Pythagoras went out on a limb when he proposed the earth was round. He had to think beyond what his five senses told him. He had to engage in a *new way of thinking* that transcended the logic of his day, knowing the world would call him crazy.

Before Pythagoras, everyone *just knew* the earth was flat. Scholars would tell you, "If you sail too far across the deep blue sea, beyond what you can see, off the edge you'll go into a bottomless abyss." However, Pythagoras would have none of that!

Are you willing to go out on a limb, as did Pythagoras? The Maestro in you loves engaging in *new ways of thinking* that transcend any prevailing logic that has you living in a flat world. In fact, the Maestro is right now urging you to sail off the edge of your comfort zone into the deep abyss, where you'll find yourself floating, free from the past, venturing forth valorously.

Your life never just happens *to* you; it unfolds as *you orchestrate* it to. You darken or make light your life, with the dim or bright opinions you hold of yourself. Your unfolding is enthralling when the Maestro is orchestrating. What treasures might you find tomorrow by stretching your mind to new dimensions today? Are you contemplating the invitation you're being offered?

> Man's mind, stretched to a new idea, never goes
> back to its original dimensions.
>
> —Oliver Wendell Holmes, Sr.[44]

The self as Maestro loves stretching your mind to marvelous new "I AMs." When you open to that, your life changes in ways that others will call you *lucky*. Do you know what *lucky* people do that *unlucky* people fail to do? They embrace themselves as the Maestro. Do you know what *unlucky* people do that *lucky* people fail to do? They embrace the *other self*, not realizing what they've done to themselves.

> Imagine your life as a game.
> What might be your aim?
> What beauty might you find
> Even in the ashes you've left behind?
>
> You can offer yourself as a gift to life.
> You can offer yourself as a problem.
> The Maestro offers you as a gift.
> The *intruder* offers you as a problem.

An osprey embryo instinctively knows her destiny is to crack free of her shell of darkness to get to the bright sunlight. When the hatchling pokes her head from the shell, an incredible new world is immediately available to her, and her sense of self is vastly superior to what she experienced just moments before. The fresh sense of self empowers the hatchling to experience her magnificence, and fly grand patterns high into the heavens.

Wow, what a thrill life can be! Not only for the osprey, but for you and me, when we poke our heads from the shell of darkness we've placed ourselves in. Can you feel yourself breaking through your shell of self-limiting opinions? Breaking through is your freedom song.

Before moving on, let's not forget The Maestro's baton.

WHAT BATON?

Do you know what you get when you've completed this expedition? Nothing... except the certainty that *you already are* what you've always wanted to be—the Maestro, fully equipped to orchestrate your life as you've always envisioned. That's when you pick up your baton.

Every Maestro has baton! Well, sure enough, you have one too! As you raise your baton to get the orchestra's attention, your renaissance begins. The moment you tap it you know with unflappable certainty, "I am the conductor," and you intuitively call forth three astonishingly resourceful states of being.

The slightest change in how you perceive yourself can make an enormous difference in how you receive yourself. Let's look at these three states of being...

chapter 19

The Dynamic Trio

RESOURCEFUL STATES OF BEING

This book is offering you pivotal moments of introspection, each chapter is adding a little more oil to your lamp of truth. Only when you stand in the bright light, beyond the shadows of the *intruder's* dark, hypnotic trance, can you become conscious of what you have unconsciously known since you were born.

When you're unconscious of something about yourself, it's like you know it's there but you aren't quite aware. What we're now uncovering will be like that for you—it feels new but you know you already knew.

Phew! There's a lot going on here.

It's time for you to step up to the podium. Pick up the baton and tap it to get your own rapt attention. You set the beat. Your heart will catch the rhythm. A gasp—a new revealing begins. You were never doomed to be a stranger to yourself. When you consciously tap the baton, you alert yourself to three resourceful states of being, always available to you.

These three states, under the conductorship of the Maestro, arouse incredible aptitudes, talents, and strengths that lay dormant within.

When you embrace these states of being, you hold yourself absolutely accountable for proving the Critical Addendum to the Ultimate Understanding.

The Dynamic Trio consists of:

The Rebel
The Recognizer
The Revealer

All three innovative states of being augment your level of participation in life. You do not learn to be the Rebel, the Revealer, or the Recognizer, you experience them directly, as they are part of your basic design as a human being.

These resourceful states appear and disappear throughout your lifetime. However, as you become more aware of the truth about yourself, you are more consciously able to call upon them. And when you allow them to perform their brilliance, your responses to your world are so productive that you even dazzle yourself with your capacity to reach those "unreachable heights."

Each state offers hallmark attributes:

THE REBEL

As the Rebel, you're not afraid to look at who you're *not*, which is the *intruder*. In fact, that becomes your firing-off point for looking at who you are—the Maestro.

In this resourceful state of heightened alertness, you are quick to catch a NO when it begins howling. Your attitude is buoyant, as you *rebel FOR* what's good and beautiful about you. I emphasized *FOR* because you don't push against the *intruder*. Your action is positive and confident without a smidgen of resentment. You simply expose the *miss-understandings* that give life to that *other self.*

Self as Rebel creates clearings for you to break free of your assumptive identity. It makes *uncomfortable* your "comfort zone of limiting beliefs."

THE RECOGNIZER

As the Recognizer, you look at yourself with fresh eyes, and you love *recognizing* and claiming quality "I AMs," to add to your *To-Be* list. This state of consciousness is a source of rejuvenation, you are continually generating new conversations for new ways of being, which offers opportunities for you to express yourself in fresh, new ways.

Self as Recognizer never agrees to the terms of the *intruder*. Nor do you succumb to your usual line of reasoning when claiming a new "I AM."

THE REVEALER

As the Revealer, you know you have to take action in the outer world if you are to maintain any ground gained in your inner world with your newly claimed "I AMs." If you did not step forward as the Revealer, the Recognizer's claim would soon fade into oblivion. Hence, you honor that claim by living into the possibilities your new "I AM" offers.

In practical terms, Self as Revealer transforms the Recognizer's noun into a verb. As Revealer, you are "outing" something about you that has been hidden. Your new "I AM" becomes an actual "way of being" for you. And how do you do that? By polishing up the new quality of character found in that "I AM," and putting it on display for the whole world to see.

These three resources—the Dynamic Trio—are skillfully inventive. As the Rebel and Recognizer you create new possibilities for yourself, and as the Revealer, you operate from these possibilities by bringing them to fruition.

ALREADY ESTABLISHED

As mentioned earlier, these three states of being—the Rebel, the Recognizer, the Revealer—are already well-established within you. You've assumed these resourceful states many times as you've grown from a child into who you are now. However, if you are to get the full benefit they offer, you must become aware of them, so you can draw on them at will.

When Self as Maestro calls upon these states, it feels like community activity, and you acknowledge all three equitably. For it's all three, working together, that make up the movement of your symphony.

Each resourceful state is designed to help bring your personal evolution to a fuller crescendo. If you leave one state out, your symphony will be incomplete.

One thing you'll quickly discover is that when you are in action as the Dynamic Trio, you experience ever-expanding feelings of satisfaction. Every higher idea of yourself that you lay claim to, opens you to new dimensions of yourself. And obviously, the more conscious you become of yourself as the Maestro and the Dynamic Trio, the easier it is to replace your assumptive identity with your authenticity.

If I am building a mountain,
and stop before the last basketful of earth
is placed on the summit, I have failed of my work.
But if I have placed even one basketful on the plain, and go on,
I am really building a mountain.

—Credited to Confucius[45]

The infinite wisdom of the Maestro and the resourceful energy of the Trio is always building a mountain. It's revolutionary! When you're struggling with a challenge and feel stopped, be still, be silent, be receptive for a moment. Not just one, but all three members of the Trio are needed to break through the dogmatic consistency of your discouraging opinions.

The walls of the *intruder* are beginning to crumble. Can you feel the rumble? In the consciousness of the Trio, "Look and Know" is the only way you go. That's when your imagined actions actually become previews of what's to come, your dreams no longer feel like foolish fantasy, and your aspirations no longer feel like sandcastles in the sky.

Whose loom weaves your visions into glorious new adventures?
Whose spindle spins the thread of those visions into new "I AMs"?

You need not look outside yourself any longer.
The Maestro is your impresario, ever ready to conduct your affairs.
The Dynamic Trio weaves and spins your visions into reality.

If you want to know what you've envisioned,
Pay attention to what you've woven and spun.

If you want to know what you can weave and spin next,
Call upon the Maestro and the Dynamic Trio.

Only the vastness offered by the ocean
Can satisfy a drop of water's appetite to know its entirety.

Only the vastness offered by the Maestro and the Trio
Can satisfy your appetite to know the entirety of humanity.

The Maestro and the Trio inspire you
To be the eager seafarer you're meant to be,
Always venturing deeper into your immensity.

It is pure rapture of the heart to know that nothing closes the gap between the world you live in and the world you would love to live in like The Maestro and the Trio.

Nothing!

The next time you reach into your dream cabinet and feel the whack of a NO, it's time to turn to The Maestro. With that simple turn, you immediately gain access to your double-edged awareness, and from that perspective the resources of the Dynamic Trio are readily available to make actual and factual all your imaginings.

> Imagination is everything.
> It is your preview of life's coming attractions.
>
> —Attributed to Albert Einstein[46]

Never mind what others do, do what is right for you! Your progress increases the more you recognize the Dynamic Trio as a dynamic force in your favor.

ME AND A PEAR TREE

When I was a kid, I was too short to reach the lower branches of our backyard pear tree, yet I never stopped dreaming about plucking those juicier pears that hung higher.

One day, while Gramps was visiting, I told him about my ambition, and how I wasn't tall enough to achieve my ideal. He put his hand on my shoulder, looked at me sternly, and asked, "Bobby, are you using all the help you can get to reach those delicious pears?"

I quickly lamented, "Yes, I've tried everything."

Gramps smiled, pointed to himself, and asked again, "Are you sure you're using *all the help* you can get?"

Then I caught on. "Will you pick me up so I can get a pear, Gramps?"

A life of just dreaming is a consequence of *not* understanding all the help you have available. You don't have the luxury of that excuse anymore. With the Maestro and the Trio you have all the help you need to reach those juicy pears on the higher branches.

The Maestro and Dynamic Trio are fully capable of freeing you from servitude to NO and WOE, but you must take full responsibility by consciously turning to them. It's but one simple shift in awareness that empowers you to claim a new "I AM," and have it fly into your life with the certainty of a bee flying to a flower, collecting pollen to make honey.

UNMATCHABLE

The Dynamic Trio are a source of unmatchable strength, laying a path to unimaginable possibilities. It begins when you can finally see that the whole of you is *not so bad after all.*

Why, it's only the movement of my eyes!
And here I've been looking for it far and wide!
Awakened at last, I find myself
Not so bad after all.

—Source unknown[47]

The Dynamic Trio loves helping you find yourself. In fact, in those enterprising states of consciousness, inch by inch it's a cinch that you'll not only find yourself but you'll find yourself to be *pretty darn good* after all.

When a storm shakes the ground under you, and thunder clamors and lightning strikes around you, let your heart open to The Maestro and his Trio. And be easy-minded about it. They are loyal servants, as devoted to your growth as are the roots of a redwood as the tree looms high into the sky.

What better way to take command of your life than to remain faithful to that which is faithful to you?

The Rebel sets things straight when a wrong self-opinion dominates.
The Recognizer claims resounding truths when you most need it.
The Revealer demonstrates what the Recognizer magistrates.

Being faithful to the Maestro and the Trio is being faithful to the Ultimate Understanding. The Maestro never lets you forget that you are a rich and majestic child of infinite intelligence. And the Trio never let you forget that you are here to reveal, feel, and share all that is good and beautiful about you.

Isn't it comforting to know that anytime you begin to feel down, you can turn to The Maestro, pick up the baton, and go to town! And rest assured, upon completion of the Trio's interplay, your spirit will soar to a great crescendo, as does the music of a symphony orchestra at the completion of a score.

The joy of going to the symphony is to enjoy the harmonious interplay of the entire orchestra. Well now, when you live as the Maestro and the Dynamic Trio, it's like having an entire orchestra traveling with you, everywhere you go.

> We lift ourselves by our thought,
> we climb upon our vision of ourselves.
>
> —Orison Swett Marden[48]

Can you think of a better way to conduct your affairs than by lifting yourself by your thoughts? Imagine envisioning yourself as you want to experience yourself, and climbing upon those visions with no hesitation. Now you know how to: simply turn to the Maestro and his Trio.

THREE

Are you familiar with the Bible verse, "For where two or three are gathered together in my name, there I am in the midst of them"?[49] I like to think of the Dynamic Trio as "the three" gathered in the name of the UU… and there stands you, in their midst—the Maestro.

Through the ages, the number three has been used to point to the significance of something new. Noah had three sons; Jonah was in the belly of the whale for three days; Jesus was resurrected on the third day. The three members of the trio repeatedly give you significant experiences of yourself in new ways. It's simply a matter of enlightened self-interest to begin thinking of yourself this way.

> When you allow the Trio to perform,
> You see howling NOs as harmless clamor,
> Like rumbling of thunder,
> And your insecure feelings vanish
> As does the morning mist in the rising sun.

No longer need you suffer at the hands of the *great pretender*. You are *not* here to be tossed about like a dry leaf in a howling wind of NO. Nor need you be tricked, any longer, by the harsh blows of lamenting WOES.

When you release the Maestro and the Trio onto the scene,
There's not a NO-Gusting or WOE-Blowing
That is strong enough to toss you about recklessly.

I hope you now have a more thorough understanding of the possibilities available when you embrace the states of the Dynamic Trio. If you're going to truly appreciate these states, it's important that you understand the specific resources, qualities, and talents that each offers.

Although all three work flawlessly together, like your heart, your lungs, and your liver, I would be doing you an injustice if I didn't give you the opportunity to study each, individually.

Let's begin by getting better acquainted with the Rebel…

chapter 20

The Rebel

A REBEL WITH A CAUSE

Self as Rebel's supreme reason for existing is to continually spark an inner revolution in the name of your evolution. In this engaging state, you are a rebel *with a cause,* always ready to dismantle any limiting decision the *intruder* is imposing.

The greatest gift you give yourself is saying, "Yes" to life. Saying "Yes" creates a clearing for new commitments and subsequent achievements. You're opening up, not closing down. The Rebel offers that gift by saying "No" to all those *miss-understandings* that say "No" to life.

As Rebel, you always seek clarity about your extraordinary nature, knowing that nothing does justice for living a great life like recovered clarity.

As the Rebel, you know that avoidance is never a solution to a problem. You know you've got to look at what you don't want in your life in order to handle it. Ergo, you look directly at a NO or WOE when it pops ups from your conditioned way of thinking.

Let the weak say, "I am strong."

—Joel 3:10 (KJV)[50]

You begin your journey of growth from weak to strong when you look at the *intruder* through the eyes of the Rebel, and declare, "That's just wrong!" And with that declaration you've set the Dynamic Trio into action.

While in this state of mind, you are very much a "doubting Thomas" but not a "pouting Thomas." Your mood is one of *inspirational* dissatisfaction, which is the vital factor that separates an optimistic doubter from a pessimistic doubter. This kind of dissatisfaction is a gift that drives your need to improve yourself so you can improve the conditions in your life.

In the consciousness of the Rebel, you doubt all limiting opinions that the *intruder* holds about you, but you don't angrily push *against* them. To rail out *against* anything angrily is to lash out thoughtlessly, which is never the spirit in which the Rebel intervenes.

As an optimistic "doubting Thomas" you are reverently *embracive* of your marvelously made nature, and never *abrasive* to the *intruder*. You hum tunes of hallelujah while editing those howling NOs that empower this *other self*; never do you sing the blues. To be a pessimistic "pouting Thomas" would be to whine and pine endlessly.

Self as Rebel is always biased in your favor, ever rebelling *for* the truth by judiciously listening for belittling self-talk. You need have no anxious concerns for yourself while in this state, for you are a natural master of intervention, calling out the *intruder's* self-limiting opinions for what they are: foolish fabrications.

BIG BLUNDER

It's a big blunder to live in ignorance and be ignorant of your ignorance. The Rebel is alert to that problem and refuses to ignore what you've been claiming you know *that just ain't so.*

> It ain't what you don't know that gets you into trouble,
> it's what you know for sure that just ain't so.
>
> —Josh Billings[51]

The reason it's important to muzzle your harmful *miss-understandings* is because you're muzzling what's muzzling *you* from bringing your many hidden talents and strengths into expression.

> When the fight begins within himself,
> a man's worth something.
>
> —Robert Browning[52]

The fight within is to flush out the truth, and the Rebel does that with the style of an aikido master. This form of martial arts is about turning the opponent's energy against himself. The Rebel is expert at denying the lies that WOES impose, by flipping the dark energy of NO into the bright light of YES.

> We shall not cease from exploration
> and the end of all exploring
> will be to arrive where we started
> and know the place for the first time.
>
> —T. S. Eliot[53]

In the state of Rebel you love setting yourself up so you might arrive where you started: a rich and majestic child of infinite intelligence. Now that you understand your disposition and attitude as the Rebel, let's look at your strategy.

CALL AN MD

Say what?

No, not a medical doctor.

Yes, a Marvelous Denial (MD).

Calling an MD is the Rebel's favorite tool of intervention. A Marvelous Denial is the act of promptly denying any lie that stops you from experiencing the UU. It's about negating the negatives that the *intruder* imposes. There is no better way to dislodge this unwanted lodger than to call an MD.

You're exercising your *Won't Power* when you call an MD. *Won't Power* arises from the Rebel's credo: "I *won't* allow the *intruder* to injure me any longer." Intervening with *Won't-Power* is using your mind to defeat the defeatist attitude the *intruder* imposes on you. The more you deny the validity of your self-limiting opinions, the less grip this *great pretender* has on you.

When you are free of the *intruder's* mental debris, what was not obvious becomes obvious: "Indeed, I am a marvelously made being!"

Your Marvelous Denials are responses from self-love; they are always healthy denials. They are like gentle *Buddha whacks,* rebutting your faulty reasoning when a NO starts howling. The driving force of a *Buddha whack* is calmness and grace, which is the style of the Rebel. Never does Self as Rebel call out a lie with the theatrics of stomping and scolding, for that surely would stir up a cantankerous WOE-Attack.

In fact, ironically, if the Rebel, were to say, "I'm MAD," it would be an acronym for "Making a Difference." That kind of madness begets gladness as you knock the whining monkey off your back.

If you're going to be judgmental, for heaven's sake, judge in your favor. That's what this is all about. Marvelous Denials are psychologically invigorating and physically energizing. And don't worry—your medical costs won't go up for calling an MD, it's free! In fact, your medical costs go down. There's less stress in your life!

Another quality found in Self as Rebel is the sense of immediacy. It's all about being present to what's happening right now—and dealing with it right now. The quicker you separate fiction from fact, the quicker the NOs collapse.

Let the dead past bury its dead.

—Henry Wadsworth Longfellow[54]

The Rebel is quick to act, so you can leave your NOs buried back there in the past where they belong. In this state, you are fully aware that if you do not let the dead past bury its dead, then yesterday's NO-Ghosts will continue to haunt you. That's when you find yourself driving down the highway of life, seeking new destination while staring fearfully in your rearview mirror. Not a good idea. Surely, you'll crash. How can you plan for a successful tomorrow when you're compelled to stare at yesterday's NOs?

(We'll cover more ground on calling an MD in Chapter 24.)

LOP AWAY

My favorite playwright had something to say about all of this. William Shakespeare, in Act 3, Scene 4, of *Richard II*, gives Gardener the line, "We lop away, that bearing boughs may live."[55] That is great advice not only for cultivating a rich vineyard of grapes, but also for cultivating a rich vineyard of thoughts to grow in one's field of consciousness.

Behind every thought of insufficiency there lies a NO, hijacking your enthusiasm. The Rebel within you is your gardener who realizes that fact, and takes full responsibility for lopping, so you may nurture thought-seeds that will grow into fruit-bearing boughs.

Shakespeare also addresses what happens if we ignore lopping away:

> Tomorrow, and tomorrow, and tomorrow,
> Creeps in this petty pace from day to day
> To the last syllable of recorded time.
>
> —William Shakespeare, *Macbeth*[56]

If a person takes the same ineffective action, day in and day out, he finds himself creeping forward at the same petty pace. Self as Rebel will have absolutely no part of that.

The perfect way to grant this robust state a powerful position in your consciousness is to grace your rebellious nature with a name. What name might you give yourSelf as Rebel? Make it personal so it lights you up.

YOUR REBEL'S NAME

When I am enjoying myself as the Rebel, I consider myself a master sculptor, forever chipping away at those layers of NOs I mistakenly piled atop my authentic essence.

Auguste Rodin, the famous French master sculptor, imagined his masterpieces buried in marble, and was an expert at chip, chip, chipping the stone away to reveal the hidden beauty. Ergo, I call myself *Rodin* when in this resourceful state, because I rejoice in chipping—calling an MD—in the fashion of that artisan.

What will you call your Rebel within: _____

DECLARATION TIME

Now you know the attitude, the mood, the personality, the philosophy, the resources, the qualities of character, as well as the strategies you use while in the highly spirited state of Rebel, it's time to declare with heartfelt enthusiasm:

I am the Rebel.
In this gifted state, I am my own psychological overseer.
My action plan is to expose the lies that hinder me from embracing the UU.

Did you make this declaration, emphatically? Movement begins when you are moved by your declaration.

Perhaps you haven't thought about it, but every single thing you do is motivated by your desire to avoid pain or to gain pleasure. The Rebel's purpose is to help you avoid pain. The next two members of the Dynamic Trio help you gain pleasure.

Let's now look at the Recognizer, the second member of the Trio…

chapter 21

The Recognizer

ERASE, THEN REPLACE

As the Recognizer, you feel electrified after the Rebel has called an MD. A Marvelous Denial creates a gap in your thought pattern, and Self as Recognizer then fills that gap by claiming a new "I AM." (Details in chapter 24.)

In this creative state you are continually issuing golden reports *about yourself to yourself*, and you are fully cognizant of the fact that all golden qualities, found in any member of the human family, are also found in you. Furthermore, you are entirely mindful of the Critical Addendum to the Ultimate Understanding: "I am destined to win at whatever I set my mind to."

> Take your practiced powers and stretch them out
> until they span the chasm between two contradictions...
> For the god wants to know himself in you.
>
> —Rainer Maria Rilke[57]

In the venturesome state of Recognizer you just love stretching out your practiced power of imagination into new dimensions so you can span the chasm between two contradictions—the Maestro and the *intruder*.

All claims you make come from an *uptown psychological position* that has you riding high with eager anticipation. Self as Recognizer is always optimistically opinionated and ready to claim a little more of all that is good and beautiful about you.

As the Rebel, you are the eraser.
As the Recognizer, you are the replacer.

As the Rebel, you dispose of what's useless.
As the Recognizer, you expose what's priceless.

As the Rebel, you take yourself out of pain.
As the Recognizer, you create opportunities for pleasure.

When you claim, "I AM" as Recognizer, you do it with such conviction that it triggers a chemical reaction in your brain, releasing endorphins into your body. The endorphins then trigger an intense *passion of will* that penetrates your entire sense of being, like a shaft of light piercing a dark room. In that state, the words you speak are electrically prompting and inspiringly moving. That's when you are able to predict your behavior with impeccable precision.

A powerful agent is the right word...
Whenever we come upon one of those intensely right words...
the resulting effect...is electrically prompt.

—Mark Twain[58]

Such power you wield when you take yourself seriously when denying a lie that a NO imposes on you, and then claim a new "I AM." In that state of alertness, the phrase *"It is finished,"* promptly arises from deep within, like molten lava rising from a volcano, which causes an intense mental impression that cannot fail to manifest as an external expression.

Example: Suppose you, as the Rebel, call an MD on the statement, "I am not talented." You call that statement out for what it is—a lie. The days of living with that lie are over. Immediately thereafter, you find yourself decreeing, like a king, "I am dripping with talent!" These words become so arousing that you vividly envision yourself demonstrating a specific talent in the field of photography or sales or piano playing...and the whole of you lights up with enthusiasm!

Self as Recognizer is willing to risk everything to cross over the valley to reach the mountain where your new claim stands. That's when you begin taking piano lessons, something you've talked about doing for years.

REDEFINE AND REDESIGN

Self as Recognizer literally redesigns your personality by redefining your identity with new "I AMs." Watch a small child give herself a complete makeover as she dresses in her ballerina costume while claiming, "I am a ballerina." It's like a million neon lights are flashing her name in the sky! Instantly, she begins dancing around the kitchen. Her mind is wide open to learning a little bit more of what she doesn't know about herself.

In moments like the above, the idea of transforming your imaginable acts into physical facts stands unchallenged. One moment the child is daddy's little girl, and the next she's a full-blown ballerina. Magical moments like that come flying back to *you* when you make claims like that child, once again.

By the way, that's the child's Recognizer at play.

Can you remember a time when you vividly imagined something new about yourself? Can you recall basking in the feeling of absolute self-assurance? You were completely absorbed and totally involved in your vision. In this venturesome state, you knew you owed nothing to darkness, and so it was natural to step into the light and claim a new you.

This one thing I do,
forgetting those things which are behind,
and reaching forth unto those things which are before,
I press toward the mark for the prize.

—Philippians 3:13 (KJV)[59]

Self as Recognizer turns your imagination into a training ground, which is the perfect inner environment for pressing forward toward the mark.

Mohammed Ali pressed toward the mark when he claimed, "*I am* the greatest." He never had to go to an ophthalmologist for corrective lenses when he envisioned himself holding the heavyweight boxing title. The feeling of irrefutability that came with his claim empowered him to score victory after victory in the ring.

Roger Bannister also pressed toward the mark when he claimed to himself, "I am a four-minute-mile breaker." He had to have claimed it or he would never have achieved such an impressive feat. Since then, there have been countless high school runners who have claimed that same victory with their own electrically prompting words…and then gone on to prove it.

What belief-barrier might you break through—what "I AM" will you make flesh—if you look at that barrier from the state of Recognizer? It's time to reclaim yourself by claiming the many "I AMs" you secretly yearn to express.

Every action has a consequence. That includes the names you choose for yourself when assuming these states of the Dynamic Trio. What name will you give yourself while assuming this restorative state? Make it personal so it turns you on.

YOUR RECOGNIZER'S NAME

I find myself intensely curious when I am Self as Recognizer. "Know thyself" is my maxim when in this state, hence, I have named this resourceful state, *Socrates.*

I love knowing Socrates is always ready to chime in when I look beyond my illusions of weakness and claim an "I AM," to come to *know myself* better.

What will you call your Recognizer within: _____

DECLARATION TIME

Now you know your strengths, your skills, your personality, your philosophy, and the other golden qualities you possess in the dynamic state of Recognizer—it's time to declare with fiery spirit:

I am the Recognizer.
In this gifted state, I rekindle an internal renaissance of new "I AMs."
My action plan is to claim the truth about myself, without exception.

You have reacquainted yourself with the two members of the Dynamic Trio that move you on the inside. And now onto the third member, that moves you on the outside…

chapter 22

The Revealer

FROM SEEING TO BEING

The Revealer lives the external reality of the Recognizer's inner narrative. When Self as Recognizer claims a new "way of being," it is *on the verge*, but it's still concealed. Self as Revealer is unconcealing what is concealed. You are "outing" and revealing the newly claimed "I AM," hence taking it from fantasy to reality.

Your creative action, as Revealer, shakes up the *poisonality* of the *intruder*. Just as a new way of seeing yourself gives you a new way of being in the world, a new way of being in the world unveils a new personality.

The combined performance of the three members of the Trio enables you to not only find yourself, but also to lose yourself—the *other self*.

Whenever you reveal a new "way of being" you occur to yourself differently. And in your newly awakened state, you make choices from today's possibilities rather than yesterday's options.

Self as Revealer's action is thrust forward by a transfiguring inner force of energy that is always creative and relentlessly purposive. There's an old Scottish proverb that says, "If wishes were horses, beggars would ride." Being wishy-washy is never an option when you're in the invigorating state of alertness, which is the Revealer's predisposition.

The Rebel denies the validity of your *miss-understandings.*

The Recognizer adds to that narrative by claiming a new "I AM."

The Revealer makes that claim real by matching it with action.

Without the externalization of your internal contemplations, your concealed "I AMs" would remain hidden. Self as Revealer's knows "If I don't act on the Recognizer's claim, I am clutching thin air and the process stops there." Hence it's in this state that you experience a deep feeling of satisfaction that far exceeds any intellectual understanding you may have when you merely ponder a new "I AM."

JUMP IN, TRY IT OUT

The act of revealing has you leaping into the unknown. It's not always predictable and Self as Revealer is okay with that because you know that the only way to reveal what was concealed about you, is to jump in and try it out.

Barring none, the strongest force found in the being of human being is our desire to express ourselves in our entirety. After losing ourselves in dazzling contemplations of new expressions, there's nothing more scintillating than turning up the flame of our desire by reaching for behavior that brings that vision to life.

Watch Diana Vishneva refining her dance steps as she reveals herself as a world-class ballerina. She dances with resolute determination that guarantees celebration. Her unyielding resolve to achieve excellence is her Revealer in full expression. Not one iota of "poor me" can be found in Diana's attitude. That's evident when she miscalculates and falters. She pauses to ponder what happened, adjusts her posture, and begins dancing once again.

In the dynamic state of the Revealer, never do you cover your eyes in fearful contemplation when it's time for action. You call forth a major strength—the superior feeling of self-assurance—and ask the question, "How much higher can I take my expression?"

Reality gives you plenty of space to evolve outwardly by expressing your inward claims, however only you can be the dauntless daredevil that says, "This is entirely up to me!" As you can see, Self as Revealer is not interested in theorizing, it's about actualizing your many merits and talents.

Children love stamping their heart's signature onto their moments of actualization. Every stamped signature is another note added to their unique orchestration. Oh, how they develop and grow so rapidly, so wonderfully! They intuitively know they are worthy of all that is good and beautiful, and they set out to prove it.

In the consciousness of Revealer, you never stop stamping your heart's signature onto such moments. In that progressive state of being you know your life is *not* meant to be a B movie. It follows that when you step up and express a new "I AM," you discipline your action with precision.

Because Self as Revealer never settles for mediocrity, when the Dynamic Trio's recital is complete, you've performed magnificently.

HELEN'S REVEALER

The Revealer in Helen Keller was in action continually. She is an outstanding example of someone who accomplished one remarkable feat after another. Despite being deaf and blind, she overcame incredible odds to achieve remarkable visions.

Among her many accomplishments, Helen was a world-renowned author, as well as a political activist and lecturer. Certainly, she knew there would be challenges, some of them mountainous, but she also knew there wasn't a mountain she couldn't climb over, walk around, or tunnel through.

Nothing happens until something moves. Helen spent her lifetime learning about her limits so she could move beyond them. When her Revealer was in action, she shook the ground beneath her, and the heavens quivered in delight.

> Life is either a daring adventure or nothing.
>
> —Helen Keller[60]

As the Revealer you see your life as a daring adventure, and the world as participatory theater. In this state you hold yourself completely responsible for the unfolding of your unique orchestration. Now I ask you, "How far are you willing to go to challenge the extent of your artistry?"

> Whatever you can do or dream you can, begin it.
> Boldness has genius, power, and magic in it!
>
> —Attributed to W. H. Murray[61]

Certainly, there will be times when you will feel like a fish out of water. However, Self as Revealer never stops demonstrating your virtues with the intention of uncovering more of yourself, which inevitably takes you to grander, new expressions of yourself. That's when you find yourself swimming through the vast ocean of life with the certainty and freedom of a dolphin.

It is the critical moment that shows the man.
So when the crisis is upon you,
remember that God, like a trainer of wrestlers,
has matched you with a rough and stalwart antagonist.
"To what end?" you ask.
That you may prove the victor at the Great Games.
Yet without toil and sweat this may not be!

—Epictetus[62]

The *intruder* is your rough and stalwart antagonist. When you hear a howling NO, the crisis is upon you. While it may take toil and sweat to face that NO, your courage grows stronger every time you turn to the Revealer to do so. In the consciousness of the Revealer, you know that if you don't seize every moment to lift yourself higher and prove yourself a victor in the Great Games of life, the *intruder* seizes the moment to pull you lower.

The transformational process from emotional revelation to physical manifestation is indeed a wondrous *relay race*, with the baton passing from the Rebel to Recognizer to Revealer.

THE RELAY RACE

The Rebel and the Recognizer set the pace; the Revealer is the third leg of this race. The Rebel runs interference; the Recognizer sets a goal with a newly claimed "I AM;" the Revealer sprints that "I AM" over the finish line with unflappable conviction.

The Dynamic Trio is truly a winning team when it comes to manifesting your dreams. To believe in yourself in new ways is outstanding. To experience yourself in new ways is astounding. What begins as fantasy ends up being reality. Every step of this process can be tested and proven by you.

Your central radiating point for feeling ready to make things right is always NOW. Worry not about tomorrow. Today is your day. Are you not one of the chosen ones? You prove that is true when *you* choose *yourself* to be a chosen one. The Revealer chants continually, "If it is to be, it is up to me!" In this state, you seal the deal when it comes to completing your personally chosen composition.

Are you ready to give this enterprising state a name? When naming the Revealer, select one that gives you a feeling of affinity with this state of being, a name that takes you beyond calculating your way through life, a name that puts you in creative command of your life.

YOUR REVEALER'S NAME

When in the state of the Revealer I consider myself a Renaissance man, hence I call myself *Leonardo*—after Leonardo da Vinci. *Leonardo* inspires creative action within me, so I might express it outwardly.

What will you call your Revealer within: _____

DECLARATION TIME

Now you know your posture, your innovative mood, the principles you live by, and the many resources you draw upon while in the authoritarian state of the Revealer—it's time to declare, with a spirit of ardent passion:

I am the Revealer.
In this gifted state I am a doer of the word, not a hearer only.
My action plan is to reveal my newly claimed "I AMs" for the world to see.

Well, now you have it. Your awareness of yourself as the Revealer makes it clear that you are the source of astounding changes in your life. The progress you make is revealed by the action you take, and the Revealer does that by always following through.

The more aware you become of what you've always unconsciously known about yourself, the more access you have to many more "I AMs." Have you jotted any more down on your *To-Be* list?

Believe it or not, you really have gotten nothing new from the past five chapters. That's because there was new nothing to get! You already had all of it. You have always been the Maestro and the Dynamic Trio!

Let's rejoice with a mental movement, spoken in a brisk, light, graceful, allegretto tempo...

chapter 23

It Takes a Lighted Candle

The Rebel offers inspirational dissatisfaction.
The Recognizer sets your compass in a new direction.
The Revealer moves with exquisite perfection.

When you find yourself failing, take time to ponder.
When you find yourself succeeding, take time to party.
Celebrate even your smallest victories.
Joyful acceptance *wills* the means for more successes.

The conviction of the Rebel inspires the Recognizer.
The conviction of the Recognizer inspires the Revealer.
The conviction of the Revealer inspires stepping higher.
Stand in the power of these convictions.

The day you stop reacting from your assumptive identity
Is the day you are free to be all you want to be.
Living freely is the greatest of all freedoms.
Dare to walk through your day giving the Maestro full play.

It takes one lit candle to light another candle.
Each candle lit lights the next candle, which lights the next.

The Maestro taps the baton, and you stand stern as the Rebel—"the terminator."
The Maestro taps again, and you stand stern as the Recognizer—"the rejuvenator."
The Maestro taps a third time and you stand stern as the Revealer—"the finisher."

The moment you tap for the Rebel, you begin your upward flight:
From denial of a lie, to claiming a truth, to presentation of proof.

Keep lighting candles until all of you lights up.
Let your world be a clearing for you to shine bright.

I am beside myself with glee. *Really!* We traveled through the thicket of the jungle of *miss-understandings* to reach this summit of the journey. This is a huge moment. The truth about yourself and your life is in clear sight.

Without the Maestro's orchestration, you continue to dwell in a barren desert of habitual reactions. With the Maestro's orchestration, that desert is transformed into a Garden of Eden.

Are you sitting in a front-row seat?
That's where the best pupils sit.
There's a seat up front for you.

Drum roll, please!
And so, without further fanfare, I am thrilled to present to you...

chapter 24

The Maestro Monologue

COMMUNICATING POWERFULLY

With our everyday preoccupation with daily affairs, we often listen to a background of conversation that does not support thinking for ourselves. If the Ultimate Understanding is to be your background of conversation, so you can fully experience the gift you are to yourself and to life, engaging in the Maestro Monologue (MM) is the way to go.

You give yourself something of extraordinary value with the MM. Something that can change your life for the rest of your life. Something no one else can do for you.

The Maestro Monologue creates a clearing for solo moments of self-reflection that free you to orchestrate your destiny as you dream it can be. There is no better way to make credible what your heart yearns in silence than to resurrect the Maestro and the Trio. The MM offers you a commanding way to address yourself by embracing those compelling states of being.

Engaging in the MM is a captivating conversation you have with yourself, about yourself, in a way that brings new meaning and purpose to your life.

With the MM, you free yourself from being who you *don't* want to be, which leaves you standing free to experience yourself as you want to be.

Learning the Maestro Monologue can feel like learning a new language. You use the same words you already use, but now you're transforming your words into *action verbs*, meaning that you speak to produce results, not to theorize, conceptualize or "talk about."

The MM places you on the primal ground upon which your *unfettered being* exist, where your life becomes an ongoing creative act that transcends those self-limiting reactions your *miss-understandings* impose on you.

By design this monologue helps you begin releasing yourself into newly claimed "I AMs" in ways that can be transformational. When you're involved in this conversation, you monopolize your attention with what it means to *be* a being with unfathomable possibilities. That's when you take resolute ownership of your life, and things begin happening organically, in your own rhythmic fashion.

It was nothing other than the troublesome monologue, imposed on you by the *intruder*, that took away your freedom to express yourself as the Ultimate Understanding. That dynasty is behind you.

Are you ready to be fearlessly human and fully transparent? The more familiar you become with the Maestro Monologue, the easier it is to distinguish truths about yourself from trifles you've been clinging to.

Imagine having a purpose in your life that is far more meaningful than what your past has offered you. That's what the MM allows you to do. You are a rich and majestic child of infinite intelligence. You are marvelously made. You are here to reveal, feel, and share all that is good and beautiful about you. Furthermore, you are destined to win at whatever you set your mind to. The MM brings all of this, front and center, and it does so conclusively.

Prepare yourself!

I now present to you…

The Maestro Monologue

It has been nothing but your own resistance that has stopped you from shining as bright as a flaming supernova. Those days are over. You are about to replace your discouraging self-talk with a priceless inner conversation that sweeps away all mental restrictions and self-harming patterns of thinking.

Here's how you pick up your baton and embrace the three resourceful states that guarantee swift progress connecting you with your original nature. There are five ingredients to the Maestro Monologue. Each ingredient becomes a fount of strength and comfort. Your intention is to experience yourself as "the source" of your experiences.

Here's a Cliffs Notes version of the five ingredients of the Maestro Monologue, to quickly familiarize you with what you're getting into:

Right curiosity begets *right awareness* (Ingredient 1).

Right awareness inspires *right rebellion* (Ingredient 2).

Right rebellion commands *rightly claimed "I AMs"* (Ingredient 3).

Rightly claimed "I AMs" motivate *right expressions* (Ingredient 4).

Right expressions prompt *joyful celebration* (Ingredient 5).

The MM is a "source document," an inner narrative that empowers you to orchestrate your eager anticipations into actual expressions. When you mix all the ingredients together, in the right order, you pave the way for the extraordinary to appear.

INGREDIENT #1
Self-Awareness

The purpose of this ingredient is to look at what's wrong so you can make it right.

This is when you embrace yourself as the Maestro, with your double-edged awareness (a quintessential element of this ingredient).

You exist as you exist because you insist what you insist about yourself. With this ingredient, you grow curious about what you *insist* about yourself. And the more curious you are, the easier it is to turn from the *intruder*, so you might turn to the breathtaking advantages the Maestro offers.

You set the stage by intentionally exploring that which threatens your personal power. Here are sample questions to awaken your double-edged awareness:

- What is it about me that constrains me from starting my own business?
- Why can't I follow through with a weight-loss program?
- What stops me from attending night school?

It's your turn. What questions might you ask yourself to pique your curiosity?

- _____
- _____
- _____

Have you finished?
Great!
Now read your questions aloud and answer them spontaneously. Don't give them any thought, simply listen to what shows up, or any pictures that may pop up in your head. Also pay attention to your tone of voice. It reveals your attitude and mood when you confront such matters.
Sample answers to my above questions:

- "I am _unqualified_ to start my own business; I _can-NOT_ afford to take risks."
  Voice tone: hopeless.
- "I am naturally fat, and that's that. I just don't have the willpower."
  Voice tone: demoralizing.
- "I am a slow learner; no sense even trying."
  Voice tone: resigned.

It's your turn. What would you say if your discouraging thought-voice has its way?

- _____
- _____
- _____

You now begin to reclaim control as you add…

INGREDIENT #2
Rebelling

The purpose of this ingredient is to intervene on your negative thought-themes.
This is when you experience Self as Rebel with your intuitive skill to call an MD. This intervention tool is a vital element of this ingredient. Your

quest is to call "faulty" those invalid conclusions you're holding onto, so you may realize all that's available beyond them.

The evolution of humanity requires we say, "There's a better way." By holding yourself accountable for what you say to yourself, you're able to intervene so you can introduce yourself to better ways of being.

Intervening effectively necessitates a healthy rebellion, which is *rebelling FOR* the truth, rather than pushing against your *miss-understandings*. Self as Rebel's "doubting Thomas" attitude gives you the resource you need to intervene successfully so you can begin a transformation of consciousness.

This ingredient makes it clear that *you* are the operative power in your life. Managing your inner conversation so you can manage your outer affairs requires a thunderous *force for* higher levels of living. This is when you jolt yourself free from those harsh judgments that stress and suppress you.

Your whole intent, with this ingredient, is to abolish self-deception when it comes to self-perception by calling out your *NOs and WOES* for the lies they imply.

Examples of calling an MD:

- "I am unqualified"—*that's a foolish lie!*
  (Why would I tell myself that?)
- "I am fat, and that's that"—*that's a ridiculous lie!*
  (It's just dumb for me to believe that.)
- "I am a slow learner"—*that's an absurd lie!*
  (I'm copping out on myself when I say that.)

It's your turn. Be sure to place yourself on "your side" and speak unflinchingly:

- _____
- _____
- _____

Remember, you're not getting into a scorching scuffle with an old NO, you're simply clearing the air of any despair. That one act immediately throws you back onto your own remarkable resources.

As you rid your inner conversations of disparaging self-opinion, you open yourself up to a revolution of new thoughts that are exhilarating and motivating. This act of peeling away what's not wanted creates the clearing you need to add the next ingredient.

That takes you to...

INGREDIENT #3
Recognizing

The purpose of this ingredient is to communicate powerfully with yourself as you claim a new "I AM."

The revealing process is a natural step after the peeling process. It's a matter of course for you to assume the resourceful state of the Recognizer after you've cleared the air of an old NO or WOE.

With ingredient #2 you *turn away* from a discouraging attitude, and with this ingredient you *turn toward* an encouraging "I AM."

Now you display your proficiency at mind-management by monopolizing your attention with what's really important to you: a correct and appropriate assessment of yourself.

At this vital crossover point you look at your assumptive identity like it's someone you once vaguely knew.

When you claim your new "I AM," you do so with a thunderbolt, first-person, present-tense statement that gives you a striking "*Aha!*" experience. This immediately gives it prominence on your *To-Be* list. Never does it occur to you to say, "I will be" or "I can be," which would leave you tottering. That's because your attitude is, "I am simply claiming what I already am, I trust what I am saying."

There is no strain when you make your claim, but rather it's like sliding into a warm jacuzzi for a long, relaxing soak. Your opportunity to experience the reality of yet another virtue or talent you possess is available, and you are taking the initiative.

Perhaps you even add a tantalizing adjective to your claim.

Examples of making your claim:

- I am outrageously qualified!
- I am remarkably *sexy* and fit!
- I am a *kick-ass* fast learner!

It's your turn, and don't forget to add a little relish to your claims:

- _____
- _____
- _____

It's with this ingredient that you nurture a feeling of conviction by nailing down what you *stand for*, after having pinned down what you *stand against*. The more you get into this, the more you'll enjoy it. A great way to put your heart into play is to tap your chest gently as you speak your claim.

Now that you've built a new platform upon which you've pledged to stand tall, it's time to move on.

You turn to…

INGREDIENT# 4
Revealing

The purpose of this ingredient is to go for it. It's about performance.

This is the "come to fruition element" of the Maestro Monologue. Now is when you eagerly seize the consciousness of the Revealer and authenticate your *spoken words* by evidencing that "I AM" in your world. Validation is indispensable to this ingredient.

There is only one rule that comes with adding this ingredient to the mix: *never leave the scene of a newly claimed "I AM" without taking a step toward revealing it.* This is where you're pledging your loyalty to that mission. Even the slightest intelligent action, demonstrated over time, confirms your intentions. Your inspired effort does not need to be something huge. However, it must come from the heart.

Imagine yourself a pilot sitting in the cockpit of an Airbus A380. As you take off, you say to yourself, "I'm responsible for all of it!" This kind of responsibility feels incredibly empowering. When you're that responsible for the steps you take to reveal a new "I AM," every move you make feels manageable.

Examples of Revealing:

- I'm taking an online business class.
- I joined the local gym and am exercising regularly.
- I signed up for night school and am learning algebra.

It's your turn. What will you do to translate your "I AMs" into valid experiences?

- _____
- _____
- _____

Quick review: with ingredients #2 and #3, you peeled away the old and proclaimed something new about you. With ingredient #4 you've validated as real what you proclaimed. By the way, whenever you do this do you know what's clearly in view? The marvelously made you, undefiled, and healthy—a pure spirit of creative energy.

This brings us to…

INGREDIENT #5
Appreciating and Celebrating

The purpose of this ingredient is to experience the true joy of thanksgiving.

Life is ever refreshing for those who take delight in their growth and expansion through appreciation and celebration. This is where you give a whopping tip to a wonderful server! You are tipping *yourself* for serving yourself so fabulously.

It's time to embrace yourself as the Maestro, and acknowledge all three resourceful states of the Dynamic Trio. Gratitude is imperative to this ingredient. Make your celebration of gratitude *yours* completely. There is no satisfaction like the satisfaction of sincere self-appreciation.

Examples of Appreciating and Celebrating:

- Softly tap on your heart and say, "Good job."
- Give yourself a big hug and treat yourself to a great cup of coffee.
- Put a big smile on your face and take time out to go to a movie.

It's your turn. How will you celebrate your victories?

- _____
- _____
- _____

With this final step, any residual resistance, lingering from prior steps, slips away.

Appreciate and celebrate—you win!

IS IT EFFECTIVE?

The life you'd love to create and the world you'd love to generate are matters of expressing *less* from your programmed nature and expressing *more* from your original nature. The Maestro Monologue is designed to help you transcend your tranquilized, obvious, programmed nature, so you can feel comfortable in the presence of the awesome truth about you.

Does the Maestro Monologue work?

You bet it does.

However, liberating yourself from your usual "ways of being" does not happen in a single leap. It takes one leap after another. The changes become more pronounced as you continue to leap, and there's no better way to do that than to practice the MM daily.

There's another bonus that comes with practicing the MM process. With each practice you roll away another stone of ignorance, until—shazam!—it's unquestionably obvious that there's nothing real about you that can be taken from you, and nothing unreal about you that can exist without your permission. That's when you know that you already are, and always have been, a rich and majestic child of infinite intelligence.

Now that you know who you are, be sure to take some time to ask, "Who will I be for others?" Don't be stingy with yourself. You are here to experience your grace by dancing in symmetry with all humanity. "The greatest among you is he who becomes the servant of all."[64] There's no better way to become a servant of all than to offer your humanness to everyone.

Humanity's external evolution depends on your internal revelations. When you grow, the entire human family grows. You not only owe it to yourself to engage in the Maestro Monologue so you may experience higher forms of your natural expressions, you owe it to all humanity.

> In proportion to the development of his individuality,
> each person becomes more valuable to himself,
> and is therefore capable of being more valuable to others.
> There is a greater fullness of life about his own existence,
> and when there is more life in the units
> there is more life in the mass....
>
> —John Stuart Mill[63]

Any time you share the Maestro Monologue with your community, you create a little space for others to experience their own inner revelations, so that *they* can contribute to the evolution of the whole human family. With that comes a greater fullness of life in the mass.

A great way to get the get the ball rolling with the MM is by counselling yourself...

chapter 25

Meet Your Mentor

IT'S YOU!

When it comes to you, no one is more qualified to engage in the Maestro Monologue than you! The MM is a tool to look beyond your conditioned awareness of yourself so you can get to the bottom of things, and it requires repetition until you've set up a new path for thinking about yourself.

Consider yourself your own mentor. Let's run through the MM again, but this time "pay attention to what you're paying attention to." Leaning on yourself is the only way to go with this.

Let's try it out. Grab your pen.

First off, can you think of a can-NOT that rules you? You got it? Okay, let's walk that can-NOT through the Maestro Monologue:

INGREDIENT #1

Self-Awareness

What specific "I can-NOT" have you given power to?
(Example: I just can-NOT learn a foreign language.)
Your turn: _____

INGREDIENT #2

Rebelling

It's time to exercise your WON'T-Power and call an MD on that limiting decision.

(Example: That's an absurd lie! I *WON'T accept* that limiting decision any longer.)

Your turn: _____

Did you exercise your WON'T-Power by being optimistically commanding, not negatively demanding? Can you feel the difference? A great way to add a little punch to this is to snap your fingers when you call the lie, "a lie!" Snap! Try it again if you didn't feel anything the first time.

INGREDIENT #3

Recognizing

Now you wobble the legs of your disempowering "can-NOT" by claiming an "I AM" that represents the opposite. Apply the principle of aikido to the process. Again, aikido is a form of Japanese martial arts where you learn to redirect the momentum of your opponent so it works to your benefit. In this case you're going to spin the negative energy of "I can-NOT" into "I CAN."

(Example: I CAN learn Spanish easily if I really want to. YES, I CAN and I WILL do that.)

Your turn: _____

Did you inject passion into the words "CAN" and "WILL"? Your power lies in your *feeeeling* the words, not speaking them. Remember, you're mentoring yourself. Go through it again if it felt feeble to you.

INGREDIENT #4

Revealing

Never leave the scene of a newly claimed, "I AM" without taking action. Action gives constancy to your claim. What will you demonstrate to validate your "I AM"?

(Example: I began my first Spanish class on Tuesday. I loved it.)

Your turn: _____

After you've acted on your new claim, it's time to express gratitude.

INGREDIENT #5

Appreciating and Celebrating

How sweet it is, knowing that *miss-understanding* is behind me.

(Example: I treated myself and my friend to lunch today.)

Your turn: _____

FIRE-BREATHING NO-DRAGONS

The impact of the MM lies in *its* simplicity and *your* immediacy. The quicker you cross the bridge from what you can-NOT do to an empowering new decision, the more effective you'll be at slaying that fire-breathing NO-Dragon.

It's wise to slay those dragons while they're only annoying, and before they start destroying. The window for optimal results is always sooner rather than later; prior to the dragon growing.

It's always easier to take care of business when you call on the MM often. It's like maintaining your ideal weight. Best you take care of business when you're a little chunky, rather than later, when you've put on 30 pounds. Correct? Well, it's the same with a howling NO. It's best to deal with it when it just begins howling, before it takes up a lot of space in your consciousness.

When practicing the MM, you always have your golden interests at heart. No longer are you taken in by fool's gold—those woeful reactions that gave you a cheap thrill, years ago. Allow no compromise when you walk a howling NO or wailing WOE through this Monologue.

Perhaps you may need to run your can-NOT through the MM a second or third time, but it never needs to be a long, involved process. However, don't be half-hearted about it!

You want to be ready when an opportunity arises to blaze a new trail toward a new vision of yourself. The next time you have an important presentation to give, a significant job interview coming up, or are considering asking that "special person" for a date—and a NO or can-NOT starts taunting you—you know what to do.

One more suggestion: every now and then, check in to see how you're doing. Simply ask:

- How did I do today?
- Did I fall back? If I did, what caused it?
- How can I refine what I did to prevent falling back again?

You've got a lot at stake here. Taking on this mission requires ruthless attention. It's not like going to a fast-food drive-through and ordering a quick-fix affirmation. Being a little hungry and looking for a half-baked solution is not enough. When practicing the MM, you cannot afford to leave out a single ingredient. Promise?

Being your own mentor will have you thinking a little more than usual about how you can best manage yourself? While in this enthusiastic state, I dare you...

chapter 26

Seven-Day Dare

MY CHALLENGE TO YOU

I challenge you, for the next *seven days*, to set up a special communication with yourself so you might reclaim and maintain your position as the Maestro. The challenge is to engage in the Maestro Monologue and call upon the Dynamic Trio continually. Make it your intention to live all *seven days* as a marvelously made being, deserving of experiencing yourself that way.

You get from this dare what you take responsibility for getting from it. Good, old-fashioned self-initiative is the way to go.

This experience will be sort of like learning to ride a bike. An instructor may explain and help you understand how to ride, but until you get on the bike, start pedaling, and learn to balance on your own, you don't know how to ride. This is your week to get on the bike and pedal.

Consider every day an opportunity to solve your problems with the aid of the Maestro Monologue. Generate enthusiasm by committing to turning all your efforts into labors of love, which is simply a matter of enjoying what you are doing. Proceed in that fashion and you will marvel at the heightened sense of flexibility and sharpness of creativity you find yourself displaying.

If for the next seven days you pledge to fully release the Maestro Monologue into everything you say and do, by day seven it will feel as natural as riding a bike. Furthermore, you'll find yourself in a superior mood because the fondness you'll feel for yourself will absolutely delight you. That's what happens when you no longer tolerate underappreciating yourself.

In the darkness of any confusion, commit to raising your lantern. With that attitude, by day five you'll find the resourceful states of the Dynamic Trio begin showing up with perfect timing, without you consciously having to call upon them. That alone will inspire you to look for opportunities, rather than looking for reasons to delay, when it comes to apply the MM to what you're doing.

HOW TO PROCEED

Start knitting, stop yawning. Be risky. Don't be timid. To engage in this dare in a lukewarm fashion would be like holding a ball of yarn in one hand and hold the knitting needles in the other, but never quite putting them together. If Self as Recognizer doesn't take action, then Self as Revealer's newly claimed "I AM" remains a ball of yarn. Don't allow this week to be unfinished knitting. By the end of it you should be wearing a beautiful sweater!

Your intention is to transform the MM into living melody, where you elevate the status of the Dynamic Trio from intellectual concepts to actual experiences. You've already proven that what you've thought about yourself in the past became your reality, and now you're proving that your new thoughts about yourself will become your new reality. This rips open space for an incredible new life.

Pledge to approach every circumstance, not nervously like a parched zebra fearing that a lion is waiting at the watering hole, but courageously and audaciously. Be radically self-reliant and rigorously fearless even in the most awkward of circumstances. The three resourceful states of the Trio are not ideals to believe in, they are commitments to throw your whole self into.

Remain vigilant to the many tricks the *intruder* will try to play, and you'll soon scare away any remaining NOs or WOES that have still been scaring you.

Consider each encounter you have with the *intruder* like peeling away layers of skin from an onion, except in this case you're peeling away layers of *miss-understandings* that empower this *other self.* Do you know what you find when you peel away the final layer of an onion? Nothing! That's also what you find when you peel away the final layer of lies that keep your assumptive identity together! And that leaves you at your center—*being* a human being—with unfathomable potential!

> How wondrous, so wondrous,
> A child of infinite intelligence you are!
> You have uncountable capacities.
>
> This is your week.
> Be unmovable when proving this.
> The starting gate is opening!

You are standing in the presence of sheer possibility. I suggest you keep a journal to record your progress.

DAYS 1 & 2
Mental Hygiene Days

Today and tomorrow you are familiarizing yourself thoroughly with the first two ingredients of the Maestro Monologue. Your intention is to face what needs facing so you can distinguish between the source that offers you beneficial truths (the Maestro), and the source that offers deception and lies (the *intruder*).

You are initiating a new practice into your routine: *briefing* and *degriefing*. You'll find it very refreshing, sort of like the oral hygiene practice of brushing and gargling to stop the march of tooth decay. Except, in this case, you are stopping the march of low self-confidence and sunken self-esteem.

Briefing is about objectively scrutinizing your subjective *miss-understandings*, knowing they are faulty programming (ingredient #1 of the MM).

Degriefing is about calling MDs on the lies contained in any NOs that start howling (ingredient #2 of the MM).

Also take a few moments daily to—chop, chop—*brief* and *degrief* your inner narrative when it's looping downward. You receive supreme insights into the nature of your self-talk when you do this.

Bring your journal with you, so you can make note of how you *briefed* and *degriefed*:

- What *miss-understandings* did you discover?
- How did you handle them?
- What did you learn?

DAYS 3 & 4
Transformation Days

This begins your hunt for newer and truer ways of seeing yourself in the world. Knowing that your struggles are not with wrong conditions in your life, but with wrong opinions you hold of yourself, now is when you pour your whole imagination into claiming new "I AMs" (ingredient #3 of the MM).

Make bagging new "I AMs" your centralizing point of power during these 48 hours, and notice how often life offers you opportunities to go beyond your usual ways of being (ingredient #4).

Remember…what you get out of these two days is what you take responsibility for getting out of them.

You are training your mind to think the way you want it to think, so your mind will treat you as you want to be treated.

> Listen for new "I AMs."
> Move those "I AMs" to deliberate "I CANS."
> Move the "I CANS" to explicit "I WILL."
> Then go for it!

Be prepared to thwart any howling NOs that try to interfere with your mission, and waste no time with any WOE for any reason. Be clear with yourself that your NOs and WOES are heat without flame and can only burn when you act lame with self-blame.

You are deep into it now. Hallelujah! Continue journaling your progress. Did you write all of your observations and insights in your journal? The wonders you seek are worth journaling about.

- What new "I AM" did you claim today and put on display?
- What old "I AM" did you replace?
- Did a howling NO appear?
- How long did you allow it to howl before calling an MD?
- Were you slack when adding any ingredient of the MM?

DAYS 5 & 6
Wizardry Days

You are now fully immersed in this *Seven-Day Dare*. Take a moment to notice the phenomenon of "accelerating acceleration." That's when you're able to, more and more quickly, affirm and accept the Maestro and the Dynamic Trio as part of your natural design.

Take time during these two days to look straight at the *intruder*. Be brash, look closely. Make a note of what you see. Might I remind you that this assumptive identity is a dark magician that takes pleasure in warring with your glorious visions.

Look even closer still. You'll discover that the *intruder* is like flimsy phyllo dough, easy to poke holes through the false assumptions of which it consists. And when you do, like phyllo dough, it quickly crumbles because there's nothing of any substance there!

The more aware you are, of the *intruder*, and of the artistry of the Dynamic Trio, the more opportunities you create for yourself to perform your wizardry. You never know what incredible "I AM" you'll pull out of the hat next!

Also, during these 48 hours, begin noticing the mind-blowing synchronicity between an "I AM" you are claiming and what occurs in your life. You'll be in awe of the genius you have tucked away when you begin giving expression to those "I AMs" you've been concealing.

> If men would steadily observe realities only,
> and not allow themselves to be deluded,
> life, to compare it with such things as we know,
> would be like a fairy tale.
>
> —Henry David Thoreau[65]

Your talents are unparalleled. You are destined to win at whatever you set your mind to. Make this experience a part of your reality during these two days.

Continue to journal your feelings and experiences.

DAY 7
Appreciation and Celebration Day

For the past six days you have felt a fire of passion stirring from within as you embraced the Maestro and the Dynamic trio. You have placed your baby toe into the great ocean of truth.

> A man on this planet cannot raise a hand
> without influencing the farthest star in the heavens
> in its unified form.
>
> —Sir James Frazer[66]

Is it possible that when you become practiced at the MM, and set your life ablaze with heavenly expressions of new "I AMs," you can raise your baton and influence the farthest star? Are you *not* part of the cosmic symphony? This is your time to feel your prominence in the universe.

Today, you are going to bask in the knowledge that it's *never, never wrong* to suspect there are always more beautiful things to discover about yourself. Your perseverance this week proven that out. While on the subject, you've also proven that it's *never, never wrong* to be suspicious of any limiting opinion you've been holding of yourself.

> You have not known what you are,
> you have slumber'd upon yourself all your life.
>
> —Walt Whitman[67]

Complete this week by reviewing all that you've written in your journal. And appreciate and celebrate the good work you've done. Give yourself a big hug as you acknowledge your accomplishments this week.

- ✓ You've nibbled sour berries in the valley. Now you are gorging heartily on the sweet fruit in the hills. Appreciate and Celebrate!
- ✓ You are enjoying a loving friendship with yourself. This friendship is your basic need answered. Appreciate and Celebrate!
- ✓ No longer are you shy to aspire higher. My goodness, you are on fire. Appreciate and Celebrate!

The more often you give yourself a hug by appreciating and celebrating all the ways you've pulled yourself up by your own bootstraps, the easier it is to see more of the *unseeable* you—that exquisite composition hidden in the depths of your being.

You'll know when you've truly mastered the Maestro Monologue—the feeling of dread is dead; no longer are you ruled by naysaying voices in your head. Life cannot help but get better when you decide there's a better way to live. That's because you know there are no limits to what you can write next in your life-script.

I'd like to bring Humpty Dumpty up for a moment, before moving on to the next chapter. It offers a touch of humor, brevity, and clarity to this human condition.

HUMPTY TOOK A TUMBLE

Charles Perrault's nursery rhyme, "Humpty Dumpty," does a terrific job of exposing the consequences of taking the NOs so seriously.

> Humpty Dumpty sat on a wall.
> Humpty Dumpty had a great fall.
> All the king's horses and all the king's men
> Couldn't put Humpty together again.
>
> — Charles Perrault[68]

Can you imagine how excited Humpty was, sitting high on that wall, looking out at his promising future, fully intending to answer that call? Then came the fall!

Or was he pushed by 60,000 NOs?!

Mother Goose, in the nursery rhyme, intimates: "Who's going to put Humpty back together again?" And she concludes that even the king's finest resources—his strongest horses and smartest men—could not do the job. The rest, she leaves to you.

If only Humpty could have avoided making the three big errors that caused him to fall—that cause all of us to fall—his life would have turned out differently.

> Error #1: Taking the NOs so seriously.
> Error #2: Coming to strong but wrong conclusions about himself.
> Error #3: Lamenting "WOE" and adopting a helpless victim role.

Clearly, had Humpty avoided the first error, he would have avoided the second one, and then there'd have been no third error to avoid.

Now that you know what pushed Humpty off the wall, you understand Humpty's plight. You also know that Humpty had to get involved in his own rescue if he was to stand tall and reclaim his position on that wall once again, where his visions of winning were available to him.

> So now I ask you, "What's next?"
> We've covered a lot of ground.
> Cinch that seatbelt even tighter.

The pearly gates to Part Four of our journey are swinging wide open. As you begin remembering everything that's true about yourself, you enter a new dimension of awareness where you witness something really quite extraordinary…

PART FOUR

thy kingdom come

chapter 27

The Kingdom of WOW

THE FRUITS OF YOUR NEW AWARENESS

A short while ago, you were reading the introduction to this book and packing for this trip. It's amazing how time flies when we're having fun! This has been an enthralling adventure. Look how far you've come. You've traveled through many states of being—all consequences of new levels of awareness.

With all that you've cognized and all you've come to recognize and realize about yourself—the fruits of your new awareness will now serve you well. Your Maestro consciousness is developed, and you find yourself standing, as the Maestro, in the Kingdom of WOW, looking forward, into your future. You are standing at the very beginning of an incredibly vibrant state of being.

Everything you have gone through has guided you to this inner kingdom, and you've arrived. Although it has always been right there in front of you.

WOW is my abbreviation for a Wonderful Obsession with Winning.

WOW has you thinking like Zeus, skyrocketing your lofty ambitions into unwavering convictions, with no doubting, no delays, no thinking small, never running away. When you allow the compelling power of WOW to flow freely, you grow exponentially. It is a stunning means of persuasion that not only astounds your nay-sayers, but literally astounds *you*.

> If we all did the things we are capable of doing,
> we would literally astound ourselves.
>
> —Thomas A. Edison[69]

When you're captivated by WOW, you love to introspect so you can recast what's possible. Your attitude is one of unsurpassable self-reliance, and even the suggestion of an insurmountable obstacle sounds preposterous. No matter how many people may tell you that something is impossible to do, you find it *impossible* to agree.

With WOW directing your attention, you surpass even the White Queen's optimistic perspective. Do you remember what she said in Lewis Carroll's *Through the Looking-Glass?* "Why, sometimes I've believed as many as six impossible things before breakfast."

The White Queen's attitude is the attitude of WOW, it opens you to more and more secrets of your heart. WOW envelopes you in a marvelous bouquet of breathtaking energy that arouses your brain chemistry, which inspires ardor, enthusiasm, and devotion to your intentions. Hence, you find yourself asking superior questions that lead to exceptional answers.

You are obsessive by nature. Are we not all? There's no escape from it. However, when you guide this inescapable force down avenues of positive expression, the less susceptible you become to thoughts that say, "It canNOT be done."

By the way, the Kingdom of WOW is not a place where you feel complete with your life. There is no completion in life. As long as you're alive, life is calling you. That's the thrill! And when possessed by the Spirit of WOW, you feel wondrously compelled to do more, so you might experience more of your aliveness.

Being wonderfully obsessed is being marvelously possessed, and there is no stopping you. That burgeoning energy for expression is the same energy found in the chrysalis from which the monarch butterfly emerges, and the same energy found in the seed of a lodgepole pinecone as it transforms into a tree of magnificent beauty. WOW invites you to know yourself that way.

WOW is *not* a system of thinking, but rather, it's a "way of being" that gives you a quantity of comfort with yourself where you find yourself in the *zone*, experiencing *flow*. That zone is where the Maestro dwells, a radically different experience than the *intruder's* survival camp—your uncomfortable comfort zone.

NOT AN ACCIDENT

WOW is never an accident. There are moments when your entanglement with the *intruder* is over, and you no longer have any interest in playing harmful psychological games with NO and WOE. In this condition of comfort you experience a conclusive state of knowing, be it consciously or unconsciously, for you are being the Maestro and have unbridled access to all of your potential. That's WOW in action.

You must be amenable to the enrapturing potency of being "Wonderfully Obsessed with Winning" if you are to naturally draw upon your many other powers, such your Power of Concentrated Attention and your Power of Intervention.

In spiritual circles many speak of the "Holy Spirit" dwelling within us. In the kingdom of WOW, it is a *wholly spirit* that captivates you, one that has you know the UU as it is meant to be known. You feel whole in the face of adversity, hence there is no sense of something missing in you as you go for a victory. With that outlook, your everyday familiarity with mediocrity quickly gives way, which makes it enjoyable and effortless to improve what you're doing.

Although I seem to be defining WOW, the only way to truly know it is to saturate your everyday affairs with it. Let's not forget the story of the woefully clucking fledgling eagle. It was the moment she was enraptured by WOW that she sensed her talons were designed for more than worm-grubbing and her wings for more than nervous flapping. WOW is what had her look high into the sky and declare, "I am an eagle," and then freely take flight to prove it.

Can you recall a time when you were wonderfully obsessed with accomplishing what you imagined? Can you remember *not* allowing yourself to rest until you brought form to your formless vision? Can you recollect any lingering fog of uncertainty immediately thinning? That's when you catapulted your high-octane aspiration into the stratosphere with unrelenting action. Do you recall such a moment?

It's always refreshing to bask in moments of recollection when your resolve was unmatchable and your confidence unshakeable. In such moments, it was WOW that opened you to the fullness of your potential, empowering you to succeed in new ways never conceptualized before.

Would that I could be the treasure-keeper and spread before you those WOW-Moments you experienced while growing up—those moments when you expressed eagerness, ardor, passion, and fervor when it came to taking action. Those were the moments when your dreams were pure, your decisions clean, and your activity exacting. In that bulletproof spirit, who could bring you to judgment and shoot down your visions of flying? No one!

What might you imagine for tomorrow if you were Wonderfully Obsessed with Winning today? The mystery of that manifestation lies *not* in your logical mind, but in your limitless imagination.

> Logic will take you from A to B.
> Imagination will take you everywhere.
>
> —Attributed to Albert Einstein

Imagination combined with WOW is a perfect mixture to break you free from your mechanical way of plodding from A to B to C. When these two notable features arise together you find yourself taking quantum leaps from A to Z.

We're often told that if we are to achieve our ambitions, we must find the right "how-to book," with the right recipe for success, or the right seminar with the right prescription for winning. Yet for so many, no matter how diligently they follow the recipe or prescription, be it for meaningful relationships, better health, more wealth, or higher spiritual fulfilment—it just doesn't seem to work. What happened?

What they didn't understand was that there is no power in a recipe or prescription, the power is in them. Or more aptly stated: "You are that power." Hence, you must work on *yourself* first if you're to apply a recipe or prescription and have it work effectively. No formula can do for you what you must do for yourself.

When you dwell in the kingdom of WOW, it's obvious that when you work on yourself first, then those promises you find in "how-to books" occur to you as credible possibilities. Now the information you gather from those books can be invaluable, and you are able to profit from what they offer, enabling you to grab the reins of your affairs and advance with increased efficiency, more and more frequently hitting your mark.

THE SECRET

The secret to rich living is always rich giving, and when living with WOW you naturally hold yourself accountable for acting honorably and generously. You have no attitude of need, no mood of greed, hence your obsession is a most valuable endowment. It has you waking up in the morning with a warm smile as you organize your day, fully intending to contribute to the betterment of everyone that passes your way. Indeed, WOW is a remarkable force of energy of great value.

> When WOW is common amongst all members of humanity,
> The affluent and the indigent will sit as one in the chambers,
> The noble and the ignoble will grace each other's tables,
> The starving and the overfed will share the same bread,
> The potent and the impotent will tear down walls of separation.
> Then all that will remain to fuss over will be:
> All the good and beautiful things we can share with one another.

The attitude of plenitude, that comes with WOW demolishes all moods of miserliness that support an inner world of barren conditions or an outer world of scarcity. Lao-Tzu, in his book, *Tao-Teh-King*, mentions that when a man abides in the *way*, his satisfactions are inexhaustible. I consider that *way* to be the "WAY of WOW." Living with the spirit of WOW is always exquisitely satisfying.

OPEN THE WINDOWS

In the days when kingdoms were how civilizations were governed, the king was the ultimate authority. There was no one higher. In your Kingdom of WOW, *you* are the ultimate authority. There is no one higher. As ruler of your kingdom, what better way could there be to transform your visions of victory into facts of triumph than to leave the windows of your mental castle wide open so you could not only let fresh air in, but also so you could toss any lingering WOES out.

WOW is not only my acronym for:
Wonderful Obsession with Winning
but also
WOW is my abbreviation for:
Woes Out the Window!

When you are *woefully* obsessed: you are dolefully possessed, and there is no starting you. However, when you are *wonderfully* obsessed you are marvelously possessed, and there is no stopping you. As much as WOE wounds, WOW heals. Consequently, with WOE gone it's never long before you're singing your victory song.

When inspired by WOW, "a mighty flame follows a tiny spark."[70] The mighty flame is your compelling obsession to ride an upward arc to victory, in a most fetching fashion. Hence, you're not actually tossing your *Woes Out the Window*, they voluntarily jump out. With the tiny spark that always precedes the mighty flame, comes the question, "Who must I *be* to ride that arc upwardly?" That question sparks you to act with precision. That's when you intuitively choose:

- Look and Know over NO-Go
- Robust curiosity over NO-It-All
- Living in flow over living with WOE-Attacks
- YES-Loops over NO-Loops
- Cannot over can-NOT

"Wait a minute, Rob" you may say, "you've said that I must clearly see the madness of WOE if I'm to rid myself of it. Well, what about Murphy's Law, which states, 'If something can go wrong, it will?' How am I to avoid that?"

MURPHY'S LAW IS WOES LAW

Murphy's Law sets WOE-Traps that pull you back repeatedly by making you react nervously. W. H. Murray, a famous Scottish mountaineer and writer, had something to say on that subject:

Until one is committed,
there is hesitancy, the chance to draw back,
and always ineffectiveness.

—W. H. Murray[71]

The lack of commitment, the hesitancy, the drawing back, and the ineffectiveness—they're all symptoms of believing in Murphy's Law, which is WOES Law. And what you believe, you make your reality.

> Rocky and slippery is the trail when WOE reigns supreme.
> Those discouraging thought-voices are blind and lame guides,
> Expert at stirring up cantankerous contemplation
> And despondent displays of exasperation.
>
> Heavenly guidance for earthly problems
> Is always available with WOW.
> Hunches come quickly, and you act on them swiftly.
> That's WOW kicking in.

In this world of polarity, if WOE has a law, then WOW must also have a law, and it does! WOW's Law states, "*If something's wrong, I can make it right.*" As much as WOE is a stopper, WOW is a starter. WOE stops you from participating in life. WOW has you excited and eager to jump in. W. H. Murray also had something to say about that.

> … then providence moves too.
> All sorts of things occur to help one
> that would never otherwise have occurred.
>
> —W. H. Murray[72]

In the spirit of WOW, you see what goes wrong as a spawning ground for new lessons to be learned and acted upon. That's when providence kicks in to assist you.

Speaking of laws, have you heard of Parkinson's Law? It states that your work expands to fill the time available for its completion. It seems, when you're WOW-Possessed, you turn Parkinson's Law upside down. In such moments, you experience time expanding to accommodate your labors, which has you feel like you're traveling miles in minutes. That's yet another perk that comes with this incomparable spirit.

It's a phenomenal journey we take, from WOE to WOW. The Merriam-Webster dictionary defines WOW as an expression of a strong feeling. I consider WOW a many splendored thing.

When you value WOW, you value winning.
When you value WOE, you value whining.

When you value WOW, you value solutions.
When you value WOE, you value drama.

When you value WOW, you value freedom.
When you value WOE, you value servitude to NO.

When you value WOW, you value self-sufficiency.
When you value WOE, you value self-deficiency.

When you value WOW, you value your inspiring daydreams.
When you value WOE, you value your nightmares.

The Maestro encourages you to call on WOW.
The *intruder* encourages you to call on WOE.

Can you see why I consider WOW a many splendored thing? If you study the nature of WOW long enough, you'll find that nature not only gifts humanity with this remarkable quality, but she also bestows all her earthly creatures with it. Let's look at the bird world for another example of WOW.

THE FLIGHTLESS GIANT

The ostrich is a bird that *cannot* fly. Does that mean it's doomed to a miserable life? Hardly! Nature graces this flightless giant with two natural aptitudes that other birds lack. The ostrich can outrun a leopard and has the punching power to break the jaw of a hyena. How's that for WOW-Power?

However, if the ostrich does not embrace the spirit of WOW upon sighting an approaching predator, do you know what happens? The bird sticks its head in the sand (actually, it lies on the ground and plays dead). Bad choice if the predator is hungry. What about the ostrich that is WOW-Possessed? It draws upon its aptitudes to save itself from tooth and claw, and few predators get the chance to pounce on it for a tasty meal.

What has the ostrich got to do with you and me?

Years ago, I arrived late at the airport only to find my Miami flight was overbooked. Everyone had boarded, and I'd been bumped. The next flight wasn't leaving until that evening. I was going to miss the wedding— and I was the best man!

I began wailing to myself, "WOE! What can I do? I'm just going to have to call and explain what happened and ask them to choose someone else to stand in for me." I was ready to stick my head in the sand and look for no other options.

Fortunately, while searching for a phone (no cell phones back then), I ran into a friend and told him of my plight. He interrupted me and said, "Rob, stop whining. Start looking for answers." Then he rushed off to catch his flight. The timing was perfect. That message was my game-changer. It struck deeply.

A surge of incredible energy shot through me, which I now identify as the spirit of WOW. I'd barely turned my attitude around before I physically turned *myself* around and ran as fast as an ostrich back to the departing gate.

It felt like the right thing to do, and sure enough, that's when *providence moved too*. A miracle happened; something too easy to explain. A passenger was feeling queasy and decided to leave the plane. Guess who was assigned that seat!

I believe this favorable change occurred because I changed my energy field by tossing my Woe Out the Window and allowing the spirit of WOW to possess me.

In the face of WOW every problem is divinely unmatched. Perhaps things won't always work out as nicely as they did in this case, but there's a good chance something magical might come of it.

Is this an exaggeration?

Not on your life!

Before moving on, I want to mention an astonishing one-syllable word that we don't use often enough. Though at first this may seem to be no more than a curious detour, I assure you it is a "prompter" that can lead directly to WOW.

OOPS

We've already covered the power of one-syllable words, like NO and WOE. Well, OOPS is another such powerful word, but this time on the bright side of the spectrum.

OOPs is a perfect replacement for NO. It's a great attitude-levitator. It's my wordplay for: "Other Options and Possible Solutions." OOPS invites the spirit of WOW into any situation.

When a child stumbles and spills her glass of milk, Mom naturally says, "OOPS, sweetie, let's clean it up together." She intuitively knows she's creating a supportive environment for the child to learn from her *miss-take*.

What if you made it a habit to say, "OOPS" when you notice someone stumbling? With this one encouraging gesture, you're offering that person the opportunity to see possibilities in place of feeling like a klutz. That one contribution can make a considerable difference.

What if, when you catch *yourself* stumbling, you make it a practice to say to yourself, "OOPS." Suppose you replace "dammit" with OOPS—just OOPS. Test it. In such moments you are a healing force for yourself.

What would the world be like if we replaced all words that knock the stuffing out of us—like NO and WOE—with words that knock the stuffing out of NO and WOE—like WOW and OOPS?

What if, instead of catching folks doing things wrong, and saying, "WOE, that was awful," we catch folks doing things right, and say, "WOW, that was great!"? What better way could there be to help each other rise above our disappointments than to remind each other we can?

Perhaps the reason dogs are called our best friends is because the moment we walk in the door, they wag their tails and bark, "Bow-WOW." Yup, a little corny, but what would it be like to treat your friends and family the way your dog treats you when you come home? What if you said, "WOW, I'm really glad to see you," and meant it?

Better still—what if you thought that way about yourself when you looked in the mirror? What could be a nobler act than that? WOW!

A couple of years ago I had printed on a T-shirt: The WOW-Factor. I still wear that T-shirt around the house to remind myself of my commitment to draw more from myself. Doing little things like this can make a big difference in your life. Never overlook the power of simplicity.

Here's one more vital piece of information to know about WOW: just as NO and WOE are partners in crime, ever stealing creative energy from your mind, WOW also has a partner, yet another remarkable advantage you possess…

chapter 28

Inspiring Addictions

CREATING RIPPLES

You are an agent of influence, and every pebble you drop into the ocean of life creates a ripple that causes a vibration. These vibrations are your contributions to this universal orchestration. To be the exquisite addition to the Grand Cosmic Symphony that you're here to be, it's important that you pay attention to what you are composing. So now let's look at one more of your advantages that drives you to compose your life as your dreams would have it. It's an impassioned craving and compelling conviction to act with precision to accomplish a particular mission. It arises from a Wonderful Obsession with Winning.

I call this captivating firepower an Inspiring Addiction (IA).

Unlike the expansive and galvanizing acceleration that comes from a Wonderful Obsession with Winning, an Inspiring Addiction is a specific, clear-cut fervor. An IA monopolizes your attention, with remarkable precision, on *one* uplifting objective. When you use this impressive asset productively, *you* decide the dominating outcome that will drive you, whereas WOW inspires you to aspire higher *always*, with *all* your endeavors.

IAs redefine your standard when you set a vision. You hold yourself accountable for achieving superbness, like one expects from a surgeon at the operating table, or an astronaut on the way to the moon. Also, when it comes to an IA, you enthusiastically choose the outcome you're intending, like deliberately creating a sweet tooth for yourself, but for something that's healthy and valuable.

Can you recall a time when you were absolutely certain that *you were certain* you'd accomplish your vision, and every ounce of your labor felt like an "art form of brilliance"? It can be anything from winning that badminton tournament, to making that big sale, or planning your spouse's surprise birthday party. Do you remember the experience of robustness and satisfaction that came with that self-assuring feeling? That feeling of gratification for what you were doing, from start to finish, was you being possessed by an Inspiring Addiction.

When you call upon this attribute, your attitude absolutely *lacks* the feeling of lack. No matter what you choose to do, a resolute feeling of undaunted decisiveness washes over you. This power is available to everyone, not just a few.

MICHELANGELO

If you've had the good fortune of viewing the ceiling of the Sistine Chapel, you've witnessed the outcome of one of Michelangelo's Inspiring Addictions. This piece of art was a colossal endeavor, and only someone Inspiringly Addicted to completing such a momentous undertaking could have expended the energy and endured the time it took. His passion for excellence inspired him to put his whole mind and body into the project until it was finished.

There's an organizing axiom behind every IA: Everything you are doing has everything to do with what you are pursuing, and there is something of value learned with every step of the process. This axiom inspires you to act willfully and pointedly even under the direst conditions.

There are as many ways to express IAs as there are rays of light pouring from the sun. When a cabinetmaker is driven by an IA, his hammering is a melodious song, and the final product is exceptionally crafted. When a mother is driven by an IA, her child-raising labors are heart-felt endeavors, and her children grow happily and healthily.

It's in your own enlightened self-interest to recognize your IAs as a rich advantage, for it is an essential element found in your storehouse of stamina. This driving force converts your commonest labor into a resourceful, uncompromising endeavor that can make a remarkable difference in your life.

> Man was born to be rich,
> or inevitably to grow rich,
> by the use of his faculties.
>
> —Ralph Waldo Emerson[73]

What aim or aspiration might prod you to call upon this faculty (IA), which is precisely what you need to give you the boost you need to take a risk and go for it? Gaining right access to this natural addictive propensity is as easy as opening a door. The first time you turned a doorknob, did you know the door would swing wide? Probably not, but it did, and you were able to make use of what was on the other side.

> Deep within man dwell those slumbering powers;
> powers that would astonish him,
> that he never dreamed of possessing;
> forces that would revolutionize his life
> if aroused and put into action.
>
> —Orison Swett Marden[74]

Ponder the exceptional wisdom found in both Emerson's and Marden's quotes. Are they saying something that sounds distantly familiar? When you stop living mechanically and unconsciously you are able to prove you were born to be rich by awakening your slumbering powers, such as WOW and IAs—forces that can revolutionize your life.

ARE YOU NOT A GIANT?

You are a giant in the land! It's a great tragedy of self-deception to sight yourself as anything less!! You feel the realness of being a giant when you dwell in the kingdom of WOW, and set your aspirations into motion with Inspiring Addictions.

However, the *intruder* is expert at using your intelligence against you by sighting you as a grasshopper, causing you to hop to and fro, nervously trying to avoid the ominous shadows of NO and WOE.

In that day there were giants in the land.
And we were in our own sight as grasshoppers,
and so we were in their sight as grasshoppers.

—Numbers 13:33 (KJV)[75]

The wisdom above was written 2,500 years ago, and is still valid today. What thou *see-est* in thyself thou *be-est* in the world, and what thou *be-est* in the world is how others see you. When you hop about nervously because of echoing NOs, you *miss-understand* yourself to be a grasshopper—and others notice!

With all that you've come to know about yourself, might I ask you now, "Who but *you* should bring judgment upon your status in life?" If you still judge yourself as a grasshopper, it's time to stop hopping, and take a leap—a leap of faith, in yourself!

There was a cartoon character, "Popeye the Sailor Man," who was around from 1919 to 1994. He was famous for gulping down a can of spinach and saying, "I yam what I yam and that's all what I yam." That's when he saw himself as a giant in the land, and took care of business. Have you yet claimed, "I yam what I yam, and all what I yam is a giant in the land?"

Compassion, courage, and integrity are pillars upon which this giant stands—all are qualities found in your authentic identity. The stature of the giant attracts golden opportunities for you to be possessed by WOW and captivated by IAs. And when you direct those compelling energies down natural channels of expression, you not only validate that you are a giant, but also that you are the Maestro when it comes to orchestrating your destiny.

Odd as it may seem, it takes tremendous energy to *maintain the illusion* that you are a grasshopper. It requires continually reacting nervously. With the might of WOW and the sway of IAs, you have an extreme advantage over any phantom grasshopper still using your field of consciousness as a hopping ground.

Again, I remind you, everything you're reading can be checked out and verified by you! Think of the relief that comes when you engage in the Maestro Monologue to prove you are a giant in the land.

Your friends will comment, "WOW, you've really changed! What happened?"

And you'll say, "Oh, the nervous grasshopper doesn't live here anymore."

WOW AND IA TOGETHER

With the background narrative of WOW supporting your self-talk, you unwaveringly decree a thing will come to pass, and then act on that decree with an Inspiring Addiction until it is finished. The more you are open to these powerful penchants, which potentiate each other, the more certain you feel that what you decree will be your reality.

Perhaps you've never thought about it this way, but I imagine you've noticed these compelling forces of energy in the personalities of great athletes, exceptional world leaders, successful inventors, and extraordinary entrepreneurs. And now you know the truth—these proclivities are also part of *your* natural makeup.

Drawing on just one of these two compelling forces is remarkable, but the combined force of this striking duo is unstoppable! That's when the winds of heaven blow in your favor.

Lay not up for yourselves treasures on earth,
where moth and rust doth corrupt,
and where thieves break through and steal;
But lay up for yourselves treasures in heaven,
where neither moth nor rust doth corrupt,
and where thieves do not break through and steal.

—Matthew 6:19-20 (KJV)[76]

WOW and IA are your treasures in heaven! When you unleash them into your life endeavors, they never betray you. However, you must *not* allow the *intruder* to pollute them, nor let NO nor WOE corrupt them. Hold them with the acclaim they deserve, so those thieves cannot break through and steal them from you.

Is this making sense?

Great!

Remain in that state.

THE SLIPPERS

Do you remember Dorothy from the much-loved movie *The Wizard of Oz?* She wore her ruby-red slippers everywhere she went. They endowed her with an incredible power, but unfortunately she didn't know it. Those magic slippers could take her home to Kansas at any moment.

Had Dorothy known that she was a giant in the land, and all she had to do was click her ruby heels together three times—tap, tap, tap—she would not have felt stuck in Oz. She could have returned home.

Tap, tap, tap—sound familiar? Is that not you—the Maestro—calling upon the Dynamic Trio?

Like Dorothy, you have that opportunity to return "home" to your marvelously made nature. All you need to do is acknowledge that you are a giant in the land and assume your rightful position as The Maestro. Now pick up that baton: tap, tap, tap.

You are an eternal dreamer. You are a remarkably creative craftsman. No longer need you roam the countryside looking for qualities and strengths you admire in others. With your newfound awareness you bring yourself back to yourself—home again!

> If I ever go looking for my heart's desire again,
> I won't look any further than my own back yard.
> Because if it isn't there,
> I never really lost it to begin with…
> There's no place like home.
>
> —Dorothy, *The Wizard of Oz*[77]

So, where do you begin? Simply turn your vision within, and you'll discover that you need never look beyond your own back yard. That is where the Kingdom of WOW and The Maestro are found.

Imagine that! All the treasures you seek have always been within reach.

When Nonoko, the Zen master, finally arrived home once again, he wrote:

> Why, it's only the movement of my eyes!
> And here I've been looking for it far and wide!
> Awakened at last, I find myself
> Not so bad after all.

Upon arriving home, you find yourself living with the same creative energy that transforms an acorn into a mighty oak tree. And as you aspire to sprout ever higher, how else could you feel but, "I'm not so bad after all"?

You can learn from truths like Nonoko offers, or you can burn from the many lies the *intruder* implies.

> Study the world less.
> Study yourself more.
>
> Dare to dream big.
> Grow into those dreams.
>
> Outgrow those dreams.
> Dream bigger dreams still.

You are at a most critical juncture in your journey. What vision of victory still dwells in fruit-bearing silence within you? You now know why so many folks live lives of quiet desperation.[78] You also know why some folks achieve their glorious aspirations.

You are no longer a novice. You have the Maestro Monologue under your belt. The spirit of WOW and the energy of IA are as much "the real deal" as the Maestro and the Dynamic Trio.

> This is it!

Treasure the thoroughness with which you've studied yourself on this journey. Allow yourself to be swept away by all that you've discovered.

> Now you get it...
> You've always had it!
> You are a rich and majestic child of infinite intelligence.
> You are a giant in the land.
> You are the Maestro!
> The Dynamic Trio are your natural resources.
> Aim for the galaxy.
> Go for the gusto.
> And gosh-darn it, don't forget to acknowledge yourself...

chapter 29

A Standing O

STANDING OVATION

William Shakespeare interprets life as living theater: "All the world's a stage, and all men and women merely players."[79] I interpret *you* as living theater! You've completed this journey. You've embraced reality. You know the authentic you, through and through. What melody will you play on the world's stage today?

> When you step onto the stage of life,
> WOE will muzzle your symphonic score.
> WOE's mood will shackle your feet to the dusty trunk,
> In the darkest corner of the stage,
> Laying you low with nowhere to go
> But to grovel in disappointing yesterdays.
>
> WOW has you center stage, eager to express yourself
> As the star performer you're here to be.
> WOW's spirit tickles your fancy with wonderful melodies.
> It inspires you to spread your arms wide,
> Yearning to explore vast regions of yourself,
> Never inquired into before.
>
> *Give yourself a Standing O!*

NO will plug the ears of your soul
With a maddening hubbub of WOE,
Throwing you into the darkness
As you hide behind the stage curtain,
Shaking with stage fright.

WOW and IAs have you feeling wonderfully obsessed,
Wonderfully possessed, and wonderfully blessed.
This tag team has you curling your toes over the edge of the stage,
As you play your melodies to your heart's content,
Knowing your life is not what it was but what you now make of it.

Give yourself a Standing O!

The deep recesses of your mind
Are no longer dungeons with gloomy turrets.
They are castles with mind-dazzling sunrises
Streaming through the windows.

Climb high on the wall of your imagination.
Allow the Ultimate Understanding to guide you.
Have faith in the Maestro Monologue.
Sings songs of praise, for you are truly a star, here to shine bright.

Give yourself a Standing O!

Your first curtain call is, *"Be True to Thyself."*
Dance and be joyous with the knowledge you hold.
You now live with wisdom rather than WOE.
Surely, your melodious songs will bring you many Broadway hits.

Your second curtain call is, *"Spread the Word."*
Share the Ultimate Understanding and the Maestro Monologue.
Help everyone to become acquainted with the Maestro within.
Everyone is a Broadway star!

Give them all a Standing O!

CLOSING THE CURTAIN

The stage curtain is coming down as we part company from this mind-expanding pilgrimage. I want to again acknowledge those many engaging thinkers from the past who have contributed enormously to this book. The wisdom and insights they offer have touched me deeply, and I hope they touched you, too.

One last time let's claim together:

THE ULTIMATE UNDERSTANDING
AND
THE CRITICAL ADDENDUM

I am a rich and majestic child of infinite intelligence.
I am marvelously made.
I am here to reveal, feel, and share
all that is good and beautiful about me.
Furthermore,
I am destined to win at whatever I set my mind to,
and
I am worthy of all that is good and beautiful.

Thank you, thank you, with all of my heart that you've allowed me to share the Ultimate Understanding, the Maestro, the Dynamic Trio, and the Maestro Monologue with you. Though I've not met most of you personally, I feel we know each other intimately. That's because we all share the same humanness.

I hope you pick this book up often and review the parts that move you. My intention for each section of this book was to take you deeper into your personal humanity. The chapter that touches you most may be a chapter that others read fleetingly. I wrote the book with the buckshot approach, offering many stories, metaphors, and exercises, not knowing which one will be the catalyst that starts a transformational shift in your consciousness.

With the Maestro Monologue, you are able to throw yourself upon your own resources a hundred times daily for further growth and expansion. I would love to hear about those experiences when the spirit of WOW occupies the inner court of your mind, and you exude confidence that brings dynamic results to your simplest acts.

Every sentence of every chapter in this book was written to help you to see the blessing you are to the world, to the galaxy, to the cosmos, to yourself. I am eternally grateful that you have taken this journey with me. May the end of this book be the beginning of your many, new, exciting travels.

Happy trails to you, until we meet again.

Rob White

How It All Began for Me

I remember that specific moment, years ago, when I was struck by the oddness of feeling *divided in two*. There I sat, feeling confident and optimistic about my future, and at the same time all caught up in the drama of life. WOW and WOE were simultaneously firing off in my mind (although I'd not labeled them yet).

That was the moment I unknowingly threw myself into an unannounced self-awareness training program, a passion that continues to enchant me today. I became intensely curious about the experience of self-contradiction—two very different attitudes with two contrasting lines of thought. Today, I can see how my curiosity evolved into an Inspiring Addiction.

I've felt like a scientist in a laboratory, studying a subject. However, what makes this fascinating for me, is that I was not only the scientist, I was also *the subject*. My ambition was to use my mind to examine my mind, and it wasn't long after diving in, that I realized how tricky that was going to be.

Being scientific about self-exploration required that I be *objective* about how *subjective* I was. There was no doubt about it, the task before me was provocative. It required that I explore beyond those treasured beliefs and lame excuses that I'd been coddling for years.

Early in my training program, I was struck by the fact that there were not only two of me, but one them was an *unwanted interloper*. Now the $64,000 dollar question became, "How did this mental boarder come to be, and does it have a lifetime lease in my mental manor?" This called for a quality of unblurred awareness and an elevated level of consciousness with which I was unfamiliar.

Things were heating up.

After countless hours of observing and contemplating this *other self*, it became obvious: *it* was nothing more than a synthesis of negative musings, faulty imaginings, and belittling self-opinions that I'd come to in moments of disappointment and distress, of which most were before age six! It was also evident that, at that age, I did not have the capacity to do a credibility report on this unwelcome tenant before *it* moved in.

At this point in my journey of self-observation I heard a battle cry from within: "Let the rebellion begin!" I'd awakened to a resourceful state of being, which I now refer to as the "the Rebel" and have named: "Rodin." Upon further examination into this *other self*—the *intruder*—I gave it yet another moniker: *the great pretender*. That was to remind myself that it had not only convinced *me* it was me, but it also convinced *everyone in my world* that it was me!

As I continued to dive deeper, I discovered that Grand Canyon of echoing NOs that have been howling on and on from years ago. With that intuitive insight I knew I'd gotten to what I now consider the main vein of the problems of humanity.

A big piece of the puzzle—solved!

Over the next several years, I began fashioning an inner narrative that helped me to develop a right relationship with my authentic self. It all started coming together: I uncovered the Ultimate Understanding, I became acquainted with the Maestro, the Recognizer, and the Revealer (the other two members of the Dynamic Trio), and I discovered the Kingdom of WOW. Then, lickety-split, I named this inner narrative, "The Maestro Monologue."

I found that the more I dug into the many dimensions of being a human being, the more I wanted to share it with the world. The next thing I knew, I was taken over by yet another Inspiring Addiction: to write this book and get it out there. This has been an incredible journey for me, to take this endeavor from A to Z.

Acknowledgments and Appreciations

Feeling grateful is a wonderfully satisfying experience. However, not sharing this experience is like putting a bow on a special moment and just letting it sit. I am thrilled to share how grateful I am…

For my wife, Kat, who taught me the inestimable value of sticking with it. She never offered me a single reason why I should quit while writing this book. Thank you, Kat, for giving me a surplus of supportive energy to reach for the galaxy and pursue my fantasy.

For Dolorez Battaglia, my mother-in-law, who through many years of dialogue together, enthusiastically encouraged me to be who I wanted to be. She helped me to come to know myself in radically new ways that have a lot to do with the contents of this book. I wish she were here to read it. Sadly, she is no longer with us.

For Shakespeare, my parrot companion and friend of 37 years. He has literally sat with me for hundreds of hours while I wrote and wrote and wrote. Shakespeare has allowed me to raise him since he was a tenderfoot chick, and while raising him, he has raised me to be patient and alert: two qualities I've drawn upon consistently while writing this book.

For the multifaceted scenery of the Jamaica Pond, and the myriad remarkable ways nature manifests herself there, especially with her flowers, trees, chipmunks, ducks, geese, and swans. I have marveled at nature's genius through many seasons. Many of my contemplations, while walking her enchanting landscape, are now crystallized in this book.

For Donna Belle, Matt Botti, Joanne Corbin, John DeNapoli, Kevin Dowd, Jack Farley, Dr. Elsa Guzman, Charlie Hubbard, Danny Kline, Rachael Kulik, Michael Lioz, Rob Lowe, Madeline Mackenzie, Monica Marlatt, Don Martin, Jonathan Mittell, Chris Moran, Ethan O'Brian,

Dr. Harris Reed, Tyrone Robinson, Deborah Rossi, Kevin Scanlon, Valerie Schechter, Dr. Phil Skerry, Ed Toner, Dawn (Sparkle) Vacek, Phil Vandersea, Dr. Amelia Weber, and Deon Williams, all who have offered me an environment of support over the many years it took me to gather and assemble the knowledge and experiences that led to writing this book.

For Tim Testa and Emma Adams, who have come on board during the editing process of this book and helped me smooth out the bumps so my message would be comfortable and direct.

For the many intuitive and innovative "everyday gurus" who traveled my way to offer an insight or tip that contributed to my personal growth, and consequently to this book.

For all you readers, who are willing to temporarily suspend your beliefs and opinions as you dive in.

Authorisms

Buddha whack: a gentle mental tap that awakens you to a new self-view.

Can-NOT: insisting *you won't* do something you actually could do if you chose to.

Dynamic Trio: three remarkably resourceful states of being (Rebel, Recognizer, Revealer).

Feeeeling: a deep meaningful heartfelt sensitivity.

Healthy Question: a question that creates space for new possibilities.

Infinite Intelligence: the purest energy in the universe that gives origin and order to everything.

IA (Inspiring Addiction): a compelling conviction to act with precision to accomplish a mission.

Intruder: that unwanted mental houseguest (the *other self*), that threatens your chances of advancing.

Look and Know: a feeling of certainty, letting you know you'll accomplish your goal.

Maestro: who you are in your finest moments while conducting your affairs in life.

MD (Marvelous Denial): denying lies impeding you from experiencing your limitlessness.

Maestro Monologue: a narrative of self-reflection that makes available your immeasurable potential.

Miss-take: an error that offers a lesson so you can refine your action for a successful retake.

Miss-understanding: an opinion you hold of yourself that misses the mark completely.

NO-Chapters: chapters in your life-story that contain howling NOs.

NO-Free: free of howling NOs.

NO-Gauges: psychological indicator lights that alert you to your NOs & WOES.

NO-Go: looking at where you want to go, convinced you'll never get there.

NO-It-All: insisting you "know it all" while arguing a negative point of view that cuts off any future possibilities.

NO-Loop: downwardly spiraling self-talk encouraged by howling NOs.

NO-Memories: NO-Tapes stored in your memory that you will listen to.

NO-Stuck: being caught in the echoes of old NOs, no matter where you go.

Other self: see *Intruder* (above).

OOPS (Other Options and Possible Solutions): a one-syllable word that silences NO.

Poisonality: I coined this hybrid word to indicate the toxicity of the *Intruder's* personality.

The Rebel: a state of being that sets things straight when wrong self-opinions dominate.

The Recognizer: a state of being that loves claiming resounding truths about you.

The Revealer: a state of being that demonstrates what the Recognizer magistrates.

To-Be **List:** your list of "I AMs" that support you with your "to-do list."

Ultimate Understanding: the undeniable, unsurpassed truth about you.

WOE (What On Earth): the cry of the helpless victim.

WOE-Attack: repeatedly moaning about your past WOES.

WOE-Stuck: caught in an attitude of "poor me."

WOE-Traps: pitfalls of self-deception that throw you in the role of "helpless victim."

Won't-Power: using your willpower to *stop* doing "what's doing you in."

WOW (Wonderful Obsession with Winning and WOES Out the Window): compelling, life-thriving energy.

Wrongly Serious: giving significance to a wrong conclusion you've come to about yourself.

YES-Loop: upwardly spiraling self-talk that lifts you to higher levels of living and giving.

Endnotes

1 Whitman, Walt. "Song of Myself." In *Leaves of Grass*. The Walt Whitman Archive, 1855.

2 Logue, Christopher. "Come to the Edge." In *New Numbers*. London: Jonathan Cape, 1969.

3 Procter, Adelaide A. "A Lost Chord." *The English Woman's Journal*, March 1858.

4 2 Kings 5:1-27 (KJV).

5 Ps. 121:1 (KJV).

6 John 15:5 (KJV).

7 Gibran, Kahlil. "On Children." In *The Prophet*. New York: Knopf, 1923.

8 1 John 4:4 (KJV).

9 De Mille, Agnes. *Dance to the Pied Piper*. Monmouthshire: Columbus Books Ltd, 1987.

10 1 Cor. 3:16 (KJV).

11 Credited to Rabindranath Tagore. Source unknown.

12 Whitman, Walt. "Song of Myself." In *Leaves of Grass*. Walt Whitman Archive, 1855.

13 Allen, James Lane. *Above Life's Turmoil*. New York: G.P. Putnam's Sons, 1910.

14 Isa. 61:3 (KJV).

15 Lucas, George, Leigh Brackett, and Lawrence Kasdan. *Star Wars Episode V: The Empire Strikes Back*. 20th Century Fox, 1980.

16 Goddard, Neville. *Be What You Wish*. Floyd, Virginia: Sublime Books, 2015.

17 Hackforth, R., trans. Plato's Philebus. Cambridge: Cambridge University Press, 1972.

18 Shakespeare, William. *Hamlet*. (1.3.78–82).

19 Cousins, Norman. Quoted in *Good Housekeeping*. 1989.

20 James 1:8 (KJV).

21 Matt. 11:15 (KJV).

22 Matt. 8:13 (KJV).

23 Cummings, E. E. "A Poet's Advice to Students." In *Miscellany*. Edited by George J. Firmage. New York: The Argophile Press, 1958.

24 Shakespeare, William. *Julius Caesar*. (1.2.140–141).

25 Carroll, Lewis. *Through the Looking-Glass.* New York: Macmillan, 1871.

26 Scott, Walter. *Marmion: A Tale of Flodden Field.* Edinburgh: Printed for Archibald Constable and Co., 1830.

27 Gabbard, Krin, ed. "Out of Notes." In *Jazz Among the Discourses.* Durham, NC: Duke University Press, 1995.

28 Arnot, William. *Roots and Fruits of the Christian Life: or Illustrations of Faith and Obedience,* 1859.

29 Steinbeck, John. *Sweet Thursday.* New York: Viking Press, 1954.

30 Shakespeare, William. *Macbeth.* (5.5.23–27).

31 Shakespeare, William. *Julius Caesar.* (2.2.32–33).

32 Shaw, George B. *Back to Methuselah: A Metabiological Pentateuch.* New York: Brentano's, 1921.

33 Fowler, H.N., trans. "Apology." In *Plato, Complete in Twelve Volumes.* Cambridge, MA: Harvard University Press, 1952.

34 Shakespeare, William. "Sonnet 30."

35 Blake, William. "Proverbs of Hell." In *The Marriage of Heaven and Hell,* 1790–93.

36 Wordsworth, William. *Lyrical Ballads.* London: J. & A. Arch, 1798.

37 Langbridge, Frederick. Source unknown.

38 de *Clairvaux, St. Bernard. Source unknown.*

39 Cohen, Alan. *I Had It All the Time: When Self-Improvement Gives Way to Ecstasy.* New York: Penguin Random House, 1995.

40 Watts, Alan. "Man in Nature." In *The Tao of Philosophy.* Clarendon, VT: Tuttle Publishing, 1999.

41 Epictetus, *Discourses of Epictetus.*

42 Matt. 25:29 (KJV).

43 Ibid.

44 Holmes, Sr., Oliver W. "The Autocrat of the Breakfast-Table." *New England Magazine,* November 1831 and February 1832.

45 Soothill, William Edward. *The Analects of Confucius.* Japan: Fukuin Printing Co., 1910.

46 Einstein, Albert. In Marshall, Gerald W. *Reaching Your Possibilities Through Commitment.* Ventura, CA: Gospel Light Publications, 1981.

47 Persona fanfiction. Source unknown.

48 Marden, Orison S. *The Victorious Attitude.* New York: Thomas Y. Crowell Co., 1916.

49 Matt. 18:20 (KJV).

50 Joel 3:10 (KJV).

51 Billings, Josh. As quoted in *Scientific American,* Vol. 31 (1874), p. 121.

52 Browning, Robert. "Bishop Blougram's Apology." *Men and Women,* 1855.

5 3 Eliot, T.S., *The Waste Land.* New York: Boni & Liveright, 1922.

54 Longfellow, Henry W. "A Psalm of Life." *The Knickerbocker*, October 1838.

55 Shakespeare, William. *Richard II* (3.4.70).

56 Shakespeare, William. *Macbeth* (5.5.19–21).

57 Mitchell, Steven, trans. *The Selected Poetry of Rainer Rilke*. New York: Random House, 1982.

58 Twain, Mark. *Essay on William Dean Howells*, 1906.

59 Phil. 3:13 (KJV).

60 Keller, Helen. *The Open Door*. New York: Doubleday, 1957.

61 Murray, W. H. *The Scottish Himalayan Expedition*. New York: Macmillan and Co., 1951.

62 Crossley, Hastings , trans. *The Golden Sayings of Epictetus with the Hymn of Cleathes*. United Kingdom: Josephs Press, 2007.

63 Mill, John S. *On Liberty*. London: John W. Parker and Son, 1859.

64 Matt. 23:11 (KJV).

65 Thoreau, Henry David. Source Unknown

66 Goddard, Neville. *The Neville Goddard Lectures, Volume 2*. 2. Vol. 2. Altenmunster, Germany: Jazzybee Verlag, 2012.

67 Whitman, Walt. *Leaves of Grass*. The Walt Whitman Archive. 1855.

68 Perrault, Charles. *The Tales of My Mother Goose: As First Collected by Charles Perrault in 1696*. California: CreateSpace Independent Publishing Platform, 2016.

69 Thomas A. Edison Quotes. BrainyQuote.com, BrainyMedia Inc, 2021. https://www.brainyquote.com/quotes/thomas_a_edison_161979, accessed February 18, 2021.

70 Dante Alighieri. *The Divine Comedy of Dante Alighieri: Inferno, Purgatory, Paradise*. New York: The Union Library Association, 1935.

71 Murray, W. H. *The Scottish Himalayan Expedition*. New York: Macmillan and Co., 1951.

72 Ibid.

73 Emerson, Ralph W. "Wealth." In *The Conduct of Life*. Boston: Ticknor and Fields, 1871.

74 Marden, Orison S. *Peace, Power, and Plenty*. New York: Thomas Y. Crowell Co., 1909.

75 Num. 13:33 (KJV).

76 Matt. 6:19–20 (KJV).

77 Fleming, Victor and King Vidor (dir). *The Wizard of Oz*. Metro-Goldwyn-Mayer Corp., 1939.

78 Thoreau, Henry D. *Walden*. Boston: Ticknor and Fields, 1854.

79 Shakespeare, William. *As You Like It*. (2.7.42–3).

CPSIA information can be obtained
at www.ICGtesting.com
Printed in the USA
LVHW110042020921
696649LV00006B/478

9 780578 875705